KETO ✦ LIFE

KETO LIFE

13-Digit ISBN: 978-1-60433-905-5

10-Digit ISBN: 1-60433-905-5

This book may be ordered by mail from the publisher. Please include $5.99 for postage and handling. Please support your local bookseller first!

Books published by Cider Mill Press Book Publishers are available at special discounts for bulk purchases in the United States by corporations, institutions, and other organizations. For more information, please contact the publisher.

Cider Mill Press Book Publishers
"Where good books are ready for press"
PO Box 454
12 Spring Street
Kennebunkport, Maine 04046
Visit us online!
cidermillpress.com

Typography: Acumin Pro, Clarendon Text Pro, Giza

Printed in China

2 3 4 5 6 7 8 9 0

KETO LIFE

OVER 100 HEALTHY AND DELICIOUS KETOGENIC RECIPES

by Sahil Makhija
of Headbanger's Kitchen

CIDER MILL PRESS

BOOK PUBLISHERS

KENNEBUNKPORT, MAINE

CONTENTS

HORNS UP,
AND WELCOME TO HEADBANGER'S KITCHEN

You're holding this book in your hands and reading it, thank you! This has been a labor of love. As of 2019, it will have been eight long years since Headbanger's Kitchen started as a whimsical metal music and food vlog on YouTube. Today, the channel is the internet's favorite resource for easy keto recipes. It's been a long journey, and I'd like to share my story with you.

WHO ARE YOU, EXACTLY?

My name is Sahil Makhija, and I'm a metal musician from Mumbai, India. For more than 18 years now, I've been the frontman of one of India's best-known metal bands, Demonic Resurrection. Sometimes I'm referred to as "Demonstealer." I know it all sounds very scary, but don't worry. Back at age 16, when I fell in love with heavy metal, I wanted to come up with the most hardcore name for myself since all my favorite musicians had them. Unfortunately, my vocabulary then only stretched so far, and Demonstealer sounded like something that would scare kids and their parents. Once the band became well-known, the name stuck.

SO, YOU'RE A MUSICIAN?

It's a long story, so stick with me. Before I became a musician, I wanted to be an actor, then a chef. Coming from a family of great cooks, it seemed fated. But music was my first love, and I pursued that relentlessly. I dropped out of college to work in a recording studio, wrote and recorded music, played tiny shows all over the country, began to play bigger gigs, and finally got a chance to play at some of the world's biggest metal festivals. But it was a hard road, one made harder by the fact that the music industry was dying. Eighteen years after I first started down this path, it felt like I'd reached the end.

WHAT DOES THIS HAVE TO DO WITH HEADBANGER'S KITCHEN?

Cooking was my other creative outlet. When bands played in my city, they would often crash at my place, and I'd cook for them. This was the kernel of an idea—why not interview a band on the show, feed them some of my cooking, and get their opinions on camera? And so Headbanger's Kitchen was born in 2011. I shot with a five-person crew and interviewed amazing bands, including Lamb of God, Gojira, and Fear Factory. It was great—except no one was watching it. My five-person crew dwindled to two, then one, then it was just me with a camera.

OKAY, BUT WHAT DOES THIS HAVE TO DO WITH KETO RECIPES?

The only thing I'd gained in all this time was, well, weight. I was always a chubby kid, and when I first started Headbanger's Kitchen, I was at my heaviest—on my 5'5" frame, I was carrying 187 pounds. Over the years, I'd tried everything from exercise to that ridiculous GM diet, but nothing stuck. Calorie counting worked for a while and brought me down to 167 pounds. Meanwhile, a former bandmate of mine seemed to have miraculously shed 66 pounds over a few months by following a mysterious diet called keto. I asked him about it, and he told me about eating bacon, cheese, meat, and nothing else. "You're going to get a heart attack and die," I told him. My then-girlfriend Deepti, though, dove deep into research on the diet, and what she found sounded too good to me. I didn't believe in it until she went on keto and I saw the difference in her. So I decided to try keto, too.

The change in my life was immediate. Not only was I losing weight consistently, I also felt better, my focus improved, I had no mood swings, no post-lunch slump, and my bloodwork numbers were great. What really irked me was that there were almost no resources on the internet for keto back in 2014, and what websites there were advocated eating bacon, butter, and Bulletproof Coffee and that was it. I knew that for a diet to be sustainable, it also had to be enjoyable, and there was no reason why keto couldn't be tasty. I started making zucchini pasta and cauliflower pizza and it was all so good that I wanted to share these recipes with the world, so I did. I did not anticipate what was going to happen next. From a mere 5,000 YouTube subscribers, the keto family grew. Today, the channel has over 200 keto recipes (and growing) and over 300,000 subscribers from all around the world.

COOL! SO WHAT'S IN THIS BOOK?

For this book, I've put together 100 of my best recipes from over the last three years of my keto life. These have all been tweaked and perfected and have brand-new photographs as well. This book has been long requested, and I've finally worked to make it happen, which is why this book is for you. Thank you for picking it up. Cheers and keep cooking!

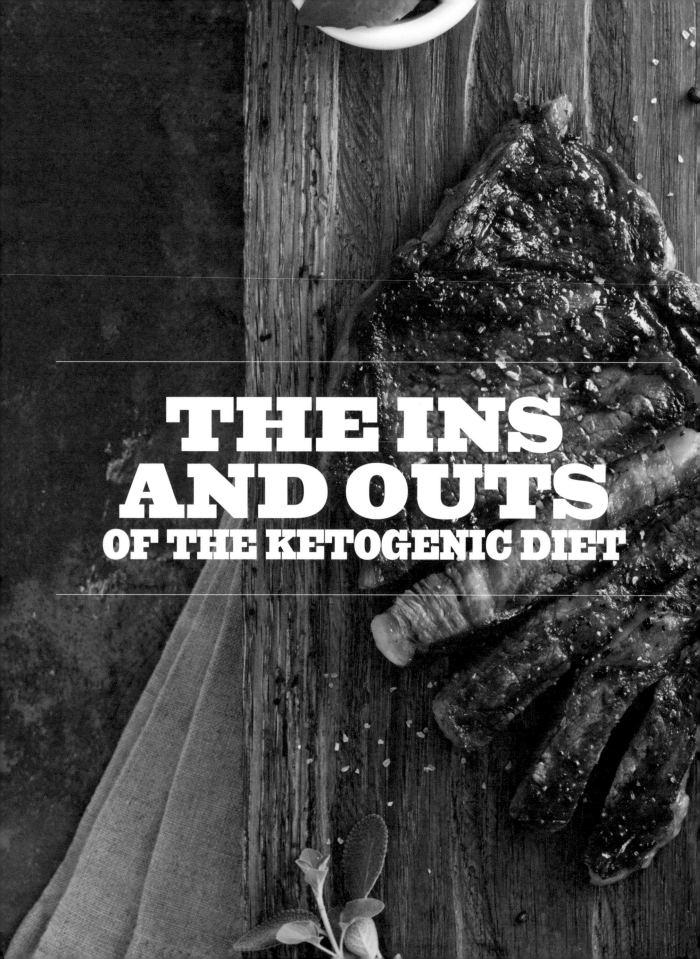

THE INS
AND OUTS
OF THE KETOGENIC DIET

WHAT IS KETOSIS?

The ketogenic diet goes by many names—low-carb high fat (LCHF), low-carb, keto—but at its heart the concept remains the same: deprive your body of carbs so it can turn to fat and stored body fat for energy through a process called "ketosis." Normally, our bodies use glucose as their primary source of energy, derived through the carbohydrates we eat. On the keto diet, we deprive our body of these carbs by limiting our consumption of them to under 20 to 30 grams in a day, or roughly 5% of our total intake of food. When this happens, our body has to find an alternate source of fuel to keep us going, and that is where ketosis kicks in and our body starts to use fat for energy. The liver converts fatty acids into ketone bodies that the brain and other organs can use as fuel.

WHAT'S SO GREAT ABOUT KETO?

Well, for starters, keto effectively turns your body into a fat-burning machine, making it a great way to lose weight, while also lowering your overall body fat. But you don't need to have a weight problem to be following the keto diet—a lot of people find that it gives them greater mental clarity, lowers cholesterol and blood pressure, and keeps them away from the processed and sugar-heavy foods that are now known to cause many diseases. When you eat high fat and moderate protein, you will also find that you are satiated and satisfied with your meals. Not craving and seeking out those between-meal snacks is half the battle! The keto diet has also been known to be very effective in helping people who suffer from diabetes, epilepsy, and a number of other autoimmune diseases. In fact, keto is not new—it was actually formulated for epilepsy patients and was found to greatly reduce the frequency and intensity of seizures. We're only now realizing the many other benefits that come from the keto lifestyle.

WHAT, EXACTLY, IS THE ROLE OF INSULIN IN KETO?

If you've been eating carbs, you're probably familiar with the post-lunch slump, that hour or two when your energy dips after you eat rice, bread, or pasta for lunch. That is due to the insulin in your body regulating the metabolism of carbohydrates and fats. After a carb-heavy meal, your pancreas produces insulin to help break down the glucose and convert it into glycogen that your body can use for energy. The insulin also triggers the production of serotonin and melatonin, which calm you down and induce sleep. But insulin is also the hormone that converts excess glycogen to body fat when your body has more carbs than it needs. When you eat carb- and sugar-heavy foods meal after meal, your insulin levels remain high for extended periods of time. Eventually, over time, your cells are unable to use the insulin effectively, leading to insulin resistance, which has been implicated in the rise of type 2 diabetes and many other autoimmune diseases. On keto, with your carb levels so low, your glucose levels aren't elevated, and your insulin doesn't spike after a meal. Lower insulin levels mean greater insulin sensitivity, cutting down on metabolic disorders and leading to effective fat burning. As a plus, you'll find you have greater mental clarity and a more stable level of energy throughout the day.

WHAT ARE MACROS AND WHY DO THEY MATTER?

"Macros" is short for "macronutrients," which is the breakdown of the components of your food. These include carbohydrates, proteins, and fats—the three components that you should keep track of on keto. Macros can be tracked through fitness apps like MyFitnessPal or Lose It!. On a keto diet, it's important to monitor your daily macros,

to ensure you're getting just enough of your daily calories from fat sources. 20 to 25% of your fat macros should come from protein, and 5 to 10% from carbohydrates, specifically net carbs. This is what will keep your body in ketosis and fat-burning mode.

WHAT ARE NET CARBS?

Most foods containing carbs have a dietary fiber or roughage component. Fiber is important for the body, because it helps with the absorption of nutrients in your gut and regulates bowel movements. A lot of dietary fiber is also insoluble and passes through your gut without being digested, so it doesn't count towards your total carb intake. Simply put, net carbs are the total amount of carbs in your food, minus the fiber. On keto, you want to keep your net carb intake between 5 to 10% of your daily calories.

WHAT KIND OF CARBOHYDRATES SHOULD MY 5 TO 10% COMPRISE OF?

When it comes to consuming carbs on the keto diet, you want those to come largely from vegetables, specifically green, leafy vegetables like spinach, kale, lettuce, chard, etc. Cruciferous vegetables like cauliflower and broccoli are high in fiber, and zucchini and eggplant are also sources of good carbs. You want to avoid starchy vegetables like potatoes, sweet potatoes, and corn—these are likely to kick you out of ketosis with just a mouthful. More colorful vegetables like peppers, tomatoes, and red onions can be consumed, but they're best eaten in moderation. It's also possible that some of your carbs might come from dairy products like cheese, so you want to read those labels carefully. All grains and grain products are off the table. You want to be especially careful with store-bought sauces and even mayonnaise—it's amazing how many hidden carbs they can have.

SO, WHAT SHOULD I BE EATING ON KETO?

Apart from the vegetables mentioned earlier, there is a whole lot to eat on the keto diet. When it comes to protein sources, you can pretty much eat any kind of meat. This includes poultry like chicken, duck, turkey, and quail; red meats like beef, lamb, pork, and venison; and also eggs of all kinds. High-fat dairy products like cream, cheese, butter, and full-fat yogurt (in moderation) are all keto-friendly, though you want to avoid milk itself as its carb count is high. Nuts are a great source of good fats, especially macadamia nuts, hazelnuts, almonds, and walnuts, but you want to be careful about eating peanuts and carb-heavy cashews in large quantities. That is why tracking macros and keeping tabs on your overall carb intake is so important. Now, since sugar is completely off the table on keto, it eliminates most fruits from the diet. However, there are a few that fall into the keto-friendly category—mainly avocadoes, and berries such as strawberries, raspberries, and blackberries. Once again, it's important to consume these in moderation in keeping with your macros. Fats, the largest component of your diet, can come from both plant and animal sources. When choosing meat, choose fattier cuts, and eat poultry with the skin on, since that's where a lot of the fat is. The other sources of pure fat are your oils, healthy ones like olive, coconut, and avocado, as well as ghee and butter. Animal fats like lard, bacon grease, and duck fat are not only healthy, but also add some serious flavor to your food.

HOW DO I KNOW WHEN I'M IN KETOSIS?

Ketosis is the state your body is in when it switches from a carb-burning to a fat-burning mechanism. In this state, your liver is actively converting fats into ketones, and these can be tracked using ketone detection strips. These strips measure the number of ketones you excrete, though it's not always an accurate measure. There are also blood ketone monitors and breath monitors, both of which are expensive and, frankly, unnecessary. The most important thing to do is to listen to your body and focus on the food and the nutrition you're getting. There are also some symptoms—like the keto flu—that mark the transition into ketosis as your body adapts to the new diet, but not everyone experiences it the same way.

WHAT IS THE KETO FLU?

As your body makes its transition from burning carbs to burning fat, it takes a few days to adapt. This can vary anywhere between 3 to 15 days depending on your body, metabolism, and insulin sensitivity. In these early days, it's not uncommon to feel a sense of malaise, some fatigue, and occasionally headaches. This is also due to the loss of electrolytes since the keto diet can be diuretic. Carbs hold on to water, and as you reduce your carb intake, your body's water retention also reduces. But don't let the keto flu scare you; it fades within a couple of days. The best way to combat it is by consuming electrolyte-rich items like soup or chicken stock; even a bouillon cube in water will work in a pinch. Most people, though, won't experience the flu at all, and will be able to transition into ketosis effortlessly.

CAN I HAVE A CHEAT DAY ON KETO?

Unlike other diets, keto is an all-or-nothing process. Eat too many carbs and you'll kick yourself right out of ketosis, and you'll have to begin the process of getting into it all over again. As a rule, it's best not to cheat at all, at least in the first month of the diet. But as your body adapts, you'll find it's easier to slip into ketosis, at which point the occasional cheat day won't hurt—they've actually been known to break a weight loss stall after a few months of keto adaptation. And though the idea of a cheat day may sound great, you'll often find that going back to processed carbs and sugar actually makes you more miserable than happy. You want to cheat responsibly, and not turn a cheat meal into a cheat day, and a cheat day into a cheat week. Cheat rarely, and cheat well, perhaps throwing complex carbs and whole grain food into your day, instead of diving headfirst into a bag of chips or a tub of ice cream.

IS ALCOHOL ALLOWED ON THE KETO DIET?

Ideally, alcohol is best avoided, as it can hamper weight loss irrespective of the diet you are on. However, occasionally you may find yourself in a social situation where you can't (or don't want to) turn down a drink. Are there keto-safe drinks? Yes. Most distilled spirits, like whiskey, white rum, Cognac, vodka, and tequila are virtually carb-free. You want to be careful with dark rum, because it can contain a significant amount of sugar. Sweet liqueurs and beers are total no-nos (even the light beers have enough carbs to swallow up your entire day's allowance), as are sugared sodas. If you must cut your drink, pick sugar-free sodas and mixers. And while you can indulge in a glass or two of dry red or white wine, it's best not to exceed that amount, given that, on average, a glass of wine contains close to 3 grams of carbs. It's also important to note that on keto, the alcohol is likely to hit you much quicker and harder and hangovers can be significantly worse because you don't have carbs to buffer them with. That's why it's essential to drink plenty of water with your alcohol. The most important thing to remember, though, is that alcohol adds empty calories to your diet, so weigh your choices carefully.

THE KETO DOS AND DON'TS

DON'T THINK OF KETO AS A MAGIC DIET

While the keto diet does turn your body into a fat-burning machine, it's important to not think it will magically make fat disappear overnight. Yes, the keto diet works faster and more visibly than some other diets, and you may initially lose more weight with it, but it's important to exercise control and stick to your macros to see results. The initial, very quick weight drop is often just water weight, so it's normal to find your weight plateauing and weight loss slowing a bit after the first few pounds. It's also important to realize that everybody is unique, so the diet will work differently for different people.

DON'T OBSESS OVER THE SCALE

Often, people get too caught up with the scale. Keto is so much more than a number on a scale; it impacts how you feel and your overall well-being. Sometimes people lose inches rather than weight while on keto; often, your body is losing fat and gaining muscle. There are various reasons the numbers on the scale may not drop, but if you are feeling good, losing inches, and overall getting the benefits of being on keto, it's best to keep the scale obsession to a minimum.

DO EAT LOTS OF REAL FOOD

On the keto diet (and in life in general), it's important to eat quality food. Fresh vegetables, meat, and dairy are so much healthier than their packaged and processed counterparts. If you eat good food, you will feel good.

DO COUNT YOUR MACROS

Being committed and having discipline definitely yields better results. It's very important to know how much you are eating and whether you are getting the right amount of fats, protein, and carbs

from the food you eat. If you aren't hitting your macros, there's a chance you'll be left hungry and craving unhealthy food. Plus, monitoring your macros makes for steadier weight loss. We've included the nutritional info by serving to make it easier for you to keep track of your macros on a meal-by-meal basis.

DO DRINK LOTS OF WATER

This cannot be stressed enough. It's extremely important to stay hydrated and drink plenty of water while you are on the keto diet. Since your body is not holding on to any water, you need to keep your reserves replenished. Drink at least ½ gallon a day, if not more. And if you don't fancy plain water, it's amazing what a slice of lime or a few cucumber slices can do to the taste.

DON'T OVEREAT

While there is a lot of debate about whether calories matter on this diet, it's important to realize that if you stuff your face and overeat, no matter what diet you're on, it won't work. If you are eating more food than your body requires, you're not helping it shed weight.

DON'T EAT PROCESSED OR PACKAGED FOOD

Most processed food isn't good for you. There's significant deterioration in the quality of macronutrients when food is overprocessed, and packaged food always has a lot of insidious, hidden carbs. It's best to eat as much fresh produce as possible and cook most, if not all, of your own food. Also, processed or packaged foods like peanut butter and mayonnaise, which are keto-friendly, are still best made on your own, as most supermarket brands will include sugar or ingredients like palm oil that you want to avoid.

DO CHECK THE NUTRITIONAL INFO OF ALL FOOD YOU EAT

Always check the nutritional labels on items before you eat them; it's important to check the nutritional label for carb content as well as for the full list of ingredients. Even with fresh produce like vegetables, if you find yourself in doubt, a quick search on the internet can help you find the nutritional information for the item. It's always better to be safe than sorry.

DO USE NATURAL, SUGAR-FREE OPTIONS

When it comes to sugar-free sweeteners, it can get pretty confusing because there are currently a lot of different options in the market. Some of these are keto-safe, like erythritol and stevia. Most others are best avoided, as they either have a high glycemic index, which can cause your insulin to spike, or are just generally deemed unhealthy. Sugar alcohols like maltitol and xylitol have high glycemic indexes and are not advised. Natural sugars like coconut sugar, agave nectar, and even honey trigger insulin just like white sugar, so they're completely off the table on this diet. It's not a big deal if you drink a diet soda with aspartame once in a while, but it's best to try and stick to more natural sugar substitutes like stevia.

DON'T GO OVERBOARD ON THE FAT

For some reason, when people think high-fat diet, they assume it's eating sticks of butter. This couldn't be further from the truth. Not only is it important to incorporate good fat sources into your diet, but when it comes to weight loss, it's also important to have an overall calorie deficit so your body can burn its own fat for fuel.

KETO STAPLES

AS WITH ANY TYPE OF COOKING, flavor is essential when eating keto. These staple flavor foundations are used in multiple recipes and are great to have on hand so meals come together faster and tastier!

SERVINGS: 20 (1 serving = 1 tablespoon)
PREP TIME: 10 Minutes
COOKING TIME: 20 Minutes

NUTRITION INFO:
(per serving)

CALORIES: 25
NET CARBS: 1 g
CARBS: 1 g

FAT: 2 g
PROTEIN: 0 g
FIBER: 0 g

BARBEQUE SAUCE

After much trial and error, I came up with a sauce that would work well for both pork and chicken, that could be made at home on the stove, and that would survive the ultimate test: an outdoor barbeque. Slather this on Bacon Bomb Balls (see page 77), toss it on pulled pork, or baste a whole roast chicken. The possibilities are endless, as is the flavor.

50 grams butter

80 grams onion

15 grams garlic

1 teaspoon salt

1 teaspoon black pepper powder

1 teaspoon paprika

1 teaspoon cayenne pepper

1 teaspoon cumin

150 grams tomatoes, diced

1 teaspoon balsamic vinegar

1 teaspoon stevia

1 teaspoon Worcestershire sauce

1 tablespoon yellow mustard

60 ml apple cider vinegar

1 tablespoon Sriracha or
hot sauce of choice

1 Melt the butter in a saucepan on a low heat and add in the onions and garlic.

2 Once the onion starts to soften, add in the salt, black pepper, paprika, cayenne, and cumin and cook for 2 minutes.

3 Next, add in the tomatoes, balsamic vinegar, stevia, and Worcestershire sauce. Cover, and cook for 7 to 8 minutes.

4 Use an immersion blender or food processor to puree the mixture until smooth.

5 Return the mixture to the saucepan, add in the mustard, apple cider vinegar, and hot sauce and cook for 5 minutes or until the mixture reaches the desired consistency.

6 Bottle and store in the fridge for up to 2 weeks.

SERVINGS: 12 (1 serving = about 15g)
PREP TIME: 2 Minutes
COOKING TIME: 2 Minutes

NUTRITION INFO:
(per serving)

CALORIES: 142
NET CARBS: 0 g
CARBS: 0 g

FAT: 16 g
PROTEIN: 2 g
FIBER: 0 g

BASIL PESTO

Pine nuts and Parmesan are not readily available (or affordable) in India. The local pesto I buy uses more parsley than basil, giving it a really distinctive flavor that inspired this basil pesto. While this recipe uses pine nuts and Parmesan, you could skip them entirely and the parsley would still amplify the umami flavor. Don't skimp on the quality of the olive oil, though—that's the one thing you should never compromise on.

30 grams Parmesan cheese, grated

20 grams pine nuts

5 grams garlic

30 grams fresh parsley

50 grams fresh basil

180 ml extra virgin olive oil

½ tablespoon fresh lemon or lime juice

Salt, to taste

1 Blend the Parmesan cheese in a blender along with the pine nuts and garlic.

2 Add in the parsley, basil, olive oil, citrus juice, and salt and blend to a smooth paste.

3 Store in the refrigerator until ready to serve.

TIP: You can also grind this recipe using a mortar and pestle for a chunky, rustic pesto.

SERVINGS: 1
PREP TIME: 5 Minutes
COOKING TIME: 1 to 2 Hours

NUTRITION INFO:

(per serving)

Consult the macros
in the bread recipe
you use.

BREAD CRUMBS

I haven't been able to get on board with breading meats with raw coconut flour or almond flour, so I decided to make my own bread crumbs. This recipe is perfect for fried chicken nuggets, fish, or anything else that needs a satisfying crunch.

1 portion of 90-Second Mug Bread (see page 35) or Coconut Flour Mug Bread (see page 40)

1   Slice the microwave mug bread and bake in an oven at 245°F for 1 to 2 hours until the bread is dry and crumbly.

2   Allow the bread to cool and then blitz in the food processor.

3   Store in an airtight container until ready to use.

SERVINGS: 7 (1 serving = 1 tablespoon)
PREP TIME: 5 Minutes
COOKING TIME: 15 Minutes

NUTRITION INFO:
(per serving)

CALORIES: 25
NET CARBS: 1 g
CARBS: 2 g

FAT: 2 g
PROTEIN: 1 g
FIBER: 1 g

TOMATO KETCHUP

The popularity of the keto diet has companies scrambling to make all kinds of sugar-free products. Meanwhile, I'm content to make my own condiments, since it allows me to control the macros. This fresh ketchup will help fill the void left by bottled, sugary versions.

10 grams garlic

300 grams tomatoes, fresh or tinned

15 grams butter

¼ teaspoon salt

¼ teaspoon white pepper

¼ teaspoon cayenne pepper

¼ teaspoon smoked paprika

1 tablespoon white vinegar

1 teaspoon soy sauce

2 drops liquid stevia

1 Blend the garlic and tomatoes together until pureed. Strain the puree to remove any seeds and pieces of skin and set aside.

2 Heat the butter in a heavy bottom saucepan until melted. Then, add in the tomato-and-garlic puree.

3 Cook for 5 to 7 minutes, stirring constantly to ensure nothing sticks to the bottom.

4 Add in all the seasonings, vinegar, soy sauce, and stevia and cook until the mixture reaches a ketchup-like consistency.

5 Remove from the heat, let cool, and serve alongside your favorite snack.

NUTRITION INFO: (per serving)	**CALORIES:** 71	**FAT:** 7 g
	NET CARBS: 1 g	**PROTEIN:** 1 g
	CARBS: 2 g	**FIBER:** 1 g

MARINARA SAUCE

Mariana is the foundation of Italian cuisine and a good marinara is integral to so many keto recipes, from pizza and zoodles (aka zucchini noodles) to chicken Parmesan and eggplant lasagna. This recipe cuts out the extra sugars and additives and adds in some fat, resulting in a keto-friendly, versatile sauce that you'll be tempted to eat right out of the jar.

2 tablespoons bacon fat or olive oil

50 grams red onion, diced

Salt and pepper, to taste

5 grams garlic, chopped

Chili flakes, to taste

400 grams tomatoes, fresh, pureed, or canned

5 grams fresh or dried oregano

A handful of fresh basil, chopped

1 tablespoon butter

1. Heat the bacon fat or olive oil in a saucepan. Once heated through, add the onion and season with salt.

2. Fry the onions for a few minutes until they turn translucent, then add in the garlic and chili flakes and cook until the onions and garlic just start to turn golden brown.

3. Add in the tomatoes and season with salt and pepper. Cover and cook for 10 to 12 minutes until the oil separates from the tomatoes.

4. Add the oregano and basil and cook for another 2 to 3 minutes. Stir in the butter and serve.

SERVINGS: 6
PREP TIME: 5 Minutes
COOKING TIME: 25 Minutes

NUTRITION INFO:
(per serving)

CALORIES: 28
NET CARBS: 3 g
CARBS: 5 g

FAT: 22 g
PROTEIN: 18 g
FIBER: 2 g

MEAT SAUCE
(RAGÙ/BOLOGNESE)

Once I made a marinara sauce to go over my favorite pizza and pasta dishes, I knew I needed to make a meat sauce to satisfy my Bolognese cravings. We're leaving the wine out of this to keep the carb counts low and adding in some fat, but otherwise this is the ragù you know and love. This sauce goes amazing over zoodles or even as part of a lasagna.

1 tablespoon olive oil

1 tablespoon butter

50 grams red onion, grated

250 grams ground beef

250 grams ground pork

Salt and pepper, to taste

Red chili flakes, to taste

Fresh or dried oregano, to taste

Leaves from a few sprigs of fresh thyme

10 grams garlic, minced

100 grams white mushrooms, chopped

100 grams tomatoes, diced

50 ml water

1 beef or chicken bouillon cube

100 grams baby spinach

100 ml heavy cream

5 grams parsley, chopped

1. Heat up the olive oil and butter in a frying pan.

2. Add the red onion to the pan and cook until translucent. Next, add in the beef and pork and stir well, breaking up the meat while stirring.

3. Season with salt, pepper, chili flakes, and oregano and cook for about 2 to 3 minutes.

4. Add in the fresh thyme and garlic and cook until the meat starts to brown.

5. Add the mushrooms, tomatoes, water, and bouillon cube to the pan. Cover and cook for 15 minutes.

6. Keep checking the sauce to make sure there is enough liquid and that nothing sticks to the pan, adding water as needed.

7. Once the sauce is nearly done, add the spinach. Cover and let wilt for 1 to 2 minutes, then finish with heavy cream and parsley.

BREADS

LET'S GET ONE THING OUT OF THE WAY—keto bread doesn't taste like real bread. Keto bread doesn't rise and stay tall and fluffy like real bread. The sooner you make peace with this, the more you will appreciate and enjoy these. Instead of gluten and yeast, we use eggs and nut flours to give the breads structure—think cake more than bread. They may be shorter and denser than carb-filled breads, but they're healthier than their gluten-based relatives and unequivocally delicious.

SERVINGS: 1
PREP TIME: 2 Minutes
COOKING TIME: 2 Minutes

NUTRITION INFO:
(per serving)

CALORIES: 324
NET CARBS: 2 g
CARBS: 5 g

FAT: 28 g
PROTEIN: 13 g
FIBER: 3 g

90-SECOND MUG BREAD

Bread is the one thing that people seem to miss the most on keto, and baking bread is a time-consuming process for people on the go. Not anymore. This bread takes less than 5 minutes to bake and can be made fresh for breakfast or to whip up a quick sandwich for lunch.

30 grams almond flour
15 grams olive oil
½ teaspoon baking powder
1 egg

1 Add all of the ingredients to a large mug and mix well.

2 Microwave the mixture for 90 seconds. Then, turn the mug over, tap it a few times, and the bread will slide out.

3 Slice the bread and eat as is or toast the pieces.

SERVINGS: 2
PREP TIME: 15 Minutes
COOKING TIME: 35 Minutes

NUTRITION INFO:
(per serving)

CALORIES: 159
NET CARBS: 4 g
CARBS: 7 g

FAT: 11 g
PROTEIN: 10 g
FIBER: 3 g

CAULIFLOWER HAMBURGER BUNS

I find that keto breads can be heavier than traditional breads thanks to their added calorie count. My quest to find a less calorie-dense bread led me to these cauliflower buns. They are the perfect keto bread to serve alongside hamburgers, and you'd never know they were made with cauliflower.

250 grams cauliflower, florets separated

Salt and pepper, to taste

25 grams Parmesan cheese, grated

30 grams cream cheese at room temperature

1 egg

1   Preheat the oven to 375°F. Grind the cauliflower florets in a food processor or grate with a box grater until they reach a couscous-like consistency.

2   Microwave the cauliflower for 5 to 7 minutes until tender, then wrap in a towel and squeeze out as much water as possible.

3   Weigh out 180 g of cauliflower after drying and mix thoroughly in a bowl with salt, pepper, Parmesan cheese, cream cheese, and the egg.

4   Divide the mixture into four portions and shape into buns, either on a parchment-lined baking sheet or a using a cookie mold.

5   Bake in the oven for 20 to 25 minutes until fully cooked and golden brown.

6   Once cooled, remove from the pan and serve.

SERVINGS: 12 (1 serving = 1 slice)	**NUTRITION INFO:**	**CALORIES:** 174	**FAT:** 15 g
PREP TIME: 10 Minutes	(per serving)	**NET CARBS:** 2 g	**PROTEIN:** 7 g
COOKING TIME: 50 Minutes		**CARBS:** 4 g	**FIBER:** 2 g

COCONUT FLOUR BREAD

It's always good to have a homemade loaf of keto bread sliced and ready in the fridge for all those times you can't be bothered to cook an elaborate meal. This loaf comes out nice and fluffy thanks to the xanthan gum and psyllium husk and is even better when toasted.

75 grams coconut flour

1 teaspoon xanthan gum

16 grams psyllium husk

1 teaspoon baking powder

½ teaspoon salt

6 eggs

100 ml olive oil

125 ml warm water

1 Preheat your oven to 335°F.

2 Line a loaf pan with parchment paper and grease thoroughly.

3 In a bowl, mix the coconut flour, xanthan gum, psyllium husk, baking powder, and salt.

4 In another bowl, whisk together the eggs and olive oil.

5 Add the dry ingredients in thirds into the egg-and-olive oil mixture, then add in the water and whisk until a batter forms.

6 Pour the mixture into the pan and bake for 40 to 50 minutes until a toothpick inserted comes out clean.

7 Remove and allow the bread to cool before removing from the pan. Slice and serve.

NUTRITION INFO:

(per serving)

CALORIES: 286

NET CARBS: 4 g

CARBS: 9 g

FAT: 24 g

PROTEIN: 8 g

FIBER: 5 g

COCONUT FLOUR MUG BREAD

Quick, what's the most common comment on my videos on YouTube? Yes, "Can this be made without eggs?" is probably first, but "Can this be made with coconut flour?" is a close second. Almond flour can get expensive as an everyday ingredient, but it's important to know that, in terms of how they behave and taste, you can't just swap coconut flour out for almond flour. This recipe is perfect for those who want an alternative to my almond flour-based mug bread (see page 35) and—dare I say it—the coconut version might be even better.

30 grams coconut flour

1 tablespoon heavy cream

1 tablespoon olive oil

1 egg

¼ teaspoon baking powder

Salt, to taste

1 Add all of the ingredients to a large mug and mix well.

2 Microwave the mixture for 90 seconds. Then, turn the mug over, tap it a few times, and the bread will slide out.

3 Slice the bread and eat as is or toast the pieces.

TIP: These breads can dry out quickly when overcooked. If your bread is too dry, microwave it for a shorter duration since your microwave might have different power settings.

SERVINGS: 6 (1 serving = 1 dinner roll)
PREP TIME: 10 Minutes
COOKING TIME: 15 Minutes

NUTRITION INFO:
(per serving)

CALORIES: 141
NET CARBS: 1 g
CARBS: 2 g

FAT: 13 g
PROTEIN: 4 g
FIBER: 1 g

DINNER ROLLS

Pav bhaji, a spicy vegetable mash mopped up with pav (a type of soft, fluffy dinner roll), is a street food favorite in Mumbai. I had a sudden craving for a plate of pav bhaji, and these rolls were born from that experiment. You can make them in a round silicone mold for that classic dinner roll shape, or just bake them in a muffin pan. They work great as a bread replacement in nearly any recipe.

50 grams cream cheese
30 grams olive oil
50 grams almond flour
½ teaspoon baking powder
Salt, to taste
2 eggs, yolks separated from whites
¼ teaspoon cream of tartar

1   Preheat the oven to 355°F. Microwave the cream cheese for 30 seconds, then add in the olive oil and whisk until emulsified.

2   Add in the almond flour, baking powder, and salt and whisk together. Allow to cool slightly, then whisk in the egg yolks.

3   In a separate bowl, add the egg whites and cream of tartar and whisk until stiff peaks form.

4   Separate the egg whites mixture into three parts, then fold into the bread mixture one at a time.

5   Pour into dome molds or baking pan of choice and bake for 12 to 15 minutes. Remove and let cool.

6   Once cooled, pop out of the molds and serve warm.

SERVINGS: 8 (1 serving = 1 cracker)
PREP TIME: 5 Minutes
COOKING TIME: 15 Minutes

NUTRITION INFO:
(per serving)

CALORIES: 88
NET CARBS: 1 g
CARBS: 2 g

FAT: 8 g
PROTEIN: 4 g
FIBER: 1 g

FATHEAD CRACKERS

The perfect vehicle for dips like Cauliflower Hummus (see page 98) and Baba Ghanoush (see page 97), these crackers are cheesy, crunchy, and egg-free, perfect for keto-safe snacking. They are great on their own and can be stored for those times when you find yourself peckish between meals.

100 grams mozzarella cheese, grated

40 grams cream cheese

Salt and pepper, to taste

1 tablespoon fresh parsley, chopped

50 grams almond flour

1   Preheat the oven to 390°F. In a large bowl, combine the grated mozzarella and cream cheese and microwave for about a minute, until the cheese is fully melted.

2   Mix well with a silicone spatula and then add the salt, pepper, and parsley and thoroughly mix again.

3   Add in the almond flour and knead together until formed into a dough.

4   Sandwich the dough between two sheets of parchment paper to prevent sticking, then roll the dough out until thin using a rolling pin.

5   Bake for 10 minutes or until golden brown. Allow the crackers to cool on a wire rack, then cut and serve warm.

NUTRITION INFO:
(per serving)

CALORIES: 86
NET CARBS: 2 g
CARBS: 3 g

FAT: 7 g
PROTEIN: 4 g
FIBER: 1 g

PEANUT BUTTER BREAD

Peanut butter is keto's magic potion. What other ingredient can partake in cookies, spreads, salad dressings, sauces, waffles, and even bread? This loaf is a nutty delight that makes the most decadent French toast.

250 grams peanut butter (natural and with no added sugar)

3 eggs

1 teaspoon white vinegar

½ teaspoon baking soda

Stevia, to taste

Pinch of salt

Butter, to grease the loaf tin

1 Preheat your oven to 335°F.

2 In a large bowl, add all the ingredients and whisk together until a dough forms.

3 Pour the batter into a greased loaf pan and bake for 25 minutes or until a toothpick inserted comes out clean.

4 Allow to cool and then remove from pan onto a cutting board. Slice and serve.

TIP: This dough is quite thick and sticky and can be hard to work with, but it comes together with a bit of elbow grease and patience.

BREAKFAST

CONVENTIONAL WISDOM SAYS BREAKFAST is the most important meal of the day. This may have been true at a time when people were eating whole-grain breads, fresh eggs, and vegetables before heading out to do physically demanding work. Today, though, most of our breakfasts start with processed carbs—white bread, cereal, sugary jams—and end with us sitting in front of a computer for 8 hours. On keto, breakfast gives you enough energy to power through your morning and keeps you full longer, so no hunger pangs and cravings will make you reach for snack packs before lunch. The recipes here aren't just for breakfast, you can eat them whenever you need a real fuel kick. Pancakes, waffles, muffins—everything you thought you couldn't eat on keto, with none of the carbs and all of the flavor and nutrition. Breakfast is truly the best meal of the day.

SERVINGS: 4 (1 serving = 1 pancake)
PREP TIME: 5 Minutes
COOKING TIME: 15 Minutes

NUTRITION INFO:
(per serving)

CALORIES: 266
NET CARBS: 3 g
CARBS: 6 g

FAT: 23 g
PROTEIN: 10 g
FIBER: 3 g

ALMOND FLOUR PANCAKES

In my house, we're firmly divided into Camp Waffle and Camp Pancake; I'm in the former, my wife in the latter. But we're agreed on one thing—both are topped with oodles of butter and maple syrup. These pancakes are nutty, fluffy, and the perfect vehicle for butter and sugar-free maple syrup.

50 grams cream cheese

50 ml heavy whipping cream

2 eggs

1 teaspoon vanilla extract

100 grams almond flour

½ teaspoon baking powder

A pinch of salt

1 teaspoon pumpkin spice mix (optional)

A few drops of stevia, powdered erythritol, or any keto-friendly sweetener

Butter, for serving

Sugar-free maple syrup, for serving

1 strawberry, sliced, for garnish

1 Melt the cream cheese in the microwave for 30 seconds and then whisk together with the heavy cream.

2 Once cool, add in the two eggs and vanilla extract and mix well.

3 Add in the dry ingredients and sweetener and mix. For a runnier batter, add more water or more heavy cream.

4 Heat a nonstick skillet and grease with olive oil, coconut oil, butter, or nonstick spray.

5 Ladle pancake batter into the skillet and cook over medium heat for 2 minutes. For fluffier pancakes, cover the skillet with a lid and let the steam cook the pancake.

6 Flip the pancakes over and cook until done.

7 Serve with butter and sugar-free maple syrup.

SERVINGS: 5 (1 serving = 1 pancake)
PREP TIME: 5 Minutes
COOKING TIME: 20 Minutes

NUTRITION INFO:
(per serving)

CALORIES: 221
NET CARBS: 3 g
CARBS: 7 g

FAT: 18 g
PROTEIN: 6 g
FIBER: 4 g

COCONUT FLOUR
PANCAKES

When I set out to make keto pancakes, I did not anticipate how good and close to the real deal these would be. The coconut flour makes a light and fluffy pancake that can be easily turned into a dessert with a dollop of sweet cream cheese frosting and dark chocolate chips.

25 grams coconut flour

½ teaspoon baking powder

½ teaspoon cinnamon

A pinch of salt

50 grams butter

50 grams cream cheese

50 ml heavy cream

3 eggs

½ teaspoon vanilla extract

2 to 3 drops stevia or low-carb sweetener of choice

Butter, for serving (optional)

Sugar-free maple syrup, for serving (optional)

Fresh berries, for serving

Sugar-free whipped cream, for serving

1 Sift the coconut flour, baking powder, cinnamon, and salt together.

2 Melt the butter and cream cheese in the microwave for 30 seconds. Then, add in the cream and whisk together.

3 Once the mixture has cooled slightly, add in the 3 eggs, vanilla extract, and 2 to 3 drops of sweetener.

4 Add the dry ingredients to the wet ingredients and whisk together until a smooth batter forms.

5 Heat a nonstick skillet and grease with olive oil, coconut oil, butter, or nonstick spray.

6 Ladle pancake batter into the skillet, cover, and cook over medium heat for 2 minutes. Flip the pancake over and cook for another 2 minutes.

7 Remove from the pan and serve with sugar-free maple syrup and butter or fresh berries and whipped cream.

SERVINGS: 1
PREP TIME: 5 Minutes
COOKING TIME: 5 Minutes

NUTRITION INFO:
(per serving)

CALORIES: 586
NET CARBS: 8 g
CARBS: 13 g

FAT: 52 g
PROTEIN: 13 g
FIBER: 5 g

ALMOND FLOUR
WAFFLES

I've always preferred savory to sweet, which is why I love using these crispy almond flour waffles as "bread" for sandwiches (or as I like to call them, wafflewiches). They make a fantastic basil pesto and mozzarella sandwich, but can also be topped with sugar-free maple syrup for a sweet treat.

50 grams almond flour

20 grams cheddar cheese, grated

4 tablespoons heavy cream

½ teaspoon baking powder

¼ teaspoon salt

A few drops of stevia

1 egg

Sugar-free maple syrup, for serving

Butter, for serving

1 Mix all the ingredients together in a bowl and whisk until a smooth batter forms.

2 Pour the batter into waffle iron and cook until golden brown.

3 Serve with syrup and butter or use to make a "wafflewich."

SERVINGS: 2 (1 serving = 1 waffle)
PREP TIME: 5 Minutes
COOKING TIME: 10 Minutes

NUTRITION INFO:
(per serving)

CALORIES: 481
NET CARBS: 7 g
CARBS: 11 g

FAT: 43 g
PROTEIN: 18 g
FIBER: 4 g

PEANUT BUTTER WAFFLES

Waffles were a lunch staple in my house growing up, not a breakfast food. Though my trusty waffle machine died a decade ago, this recipe inspired me to buy another and revisit my childhood memories. These waffles are as good as—if not better than—regular flour waffles, and the peanut butter adds a delicious background nuttiness.

80 grams peanut butter
(natural and with no added sugar)

15 grams butter

40 grams cream cheese

40 ml heavy cream

½ teaspoon baking powder

Stevia or keto-friendly sweetener
of choice, to taste

2 eggs

Sugar-free maple syrup, for serving

Butter, for serving

1 Microwave the peanut butter, butter, and cream cheese in a bowl for 30 seconds and mix well. Next, add in the cream, baking powder, and sweetener and mix well.

2 Finally, add in the eggs and mix well until it forms a batter. The peanut butter batter will be thicker than normal pancake batter.

3 Ladle the batter into a waffle maker and cook until crisp and golden brown on the outside, about 2 to 3 minutes.

4 Serve with sugar-free maple syrup and butter.

SERVINGS: 8 (1 serving = 1 muffin)
PREP TIME: 10 Minutes
COOKING TIME: 30 Minutes

NUTRITION INFO:
(per serving)

CALORIES: 226
NET CARBS: 3 g
CARBS: 3 g

FAT: 21 g
PROTEIN: 7 g
FIBER: 2 g

LEMON AND POPPY SEED MUFFINS

The zing of lemon and the crunchiness of black poppy seeds elevate an ordinary breakfast muffin into something that's more dessert than a meal. These muffins can be made ahead and frozen, so you can defrost one when you need it. They're also a great snack between meals.

140 grams almond flour

1½ tablespoons poppy seeds

½ teaspoon baking powder

Salt, to taste

Juice and zest of 1 lemon

85 grams butter

100 grams Sukrin Gold or keto-friendly sweetener of choice

85 grams sour cream

½ teaspoon vanilla extract

2 eggs

1   Preheat your oven to 345°F.

2   Combine the almond flour, poppy seeds, baking powder, salt, and lemon zest in a bowl and mix together with a fork.

3   In another bowl, cream together the butter and sweetener. If using a granulated sweetener, pulse 3 or 4 times in the blender before adding to make it easier to dissolve.

4   Add the sour cream to the butter mix and whisk together, then add in the vanilla, eggs, and lemon juice and whisk together. It is normal for the mixture to appear curdled.

5   Add the dry ingredients to the wet and whisk until it forms a smooth batter.

6   Pour the batter into a lined cupcake or muffin pan, filling each compartment only ⅔ of the way up. Then, bake for about 25 to 30 minutes or until a toothpick inserted comes out clean.

7   Remove from the oven and let the muffins cool for 20 minutes before serving.

SERVINGS: 1	**NUTRITION INFO:**	**CALORIES:** 360	**FAT:** 34 g
PREP TIME: 2 Minutes	(per serving)	**NET CARBS:** 1 g	**PROTEIN:** 13 g
COOKING TIME: 10 Minutes		**CARBS:** 1 g	**FIBER:** 0 g

BROWN BUTTER SCRAMBLED EGGS

Brown butter is a sauce cooked from butter and sometimes flavored with herbs, vinegar, capers, or other ingredients. Once I tried it for myself, I knew I had to whip up a savory breakfast with it. Since eggs are a keto staple and there's always room for a new and delicious way to cook eggs, this dish found its way onto my breakfast menu immediately.

2 eggs

30 grams butter

Salt and pepper, to taste

Fresh chives, diced

Keto-friendly bread, for serving (optional)

1 Beat the two eggs in a bowl and set aside.

2 Melt the butter in a frying pan and cook until the butter turns a nutty brown color.

3 Turn down the heat to the lowest setting and add in the eggs, stirring constantly until scrambled.

4 Season with salt and pepper, top with chives, and serve with a slice of keto-friendly bread or as is.

NUTRITION INFO:
(per serving)

CALORIES: 241
NET CARBS: 1 g
CARBS: 1 g

FAT: 22 g
PROTEIN: 10 g
FIBER: 0 g

CHEESY FRIED EGGS THREE WAYS

My wife got on keto before me, and she was eating eggs for breakfast most days, and getting bored of them just as fast. I was always looking for ways to make eggs great again, and realized the best part of a cheese omelet was all the melted cheese that would brown and crisp up around it. These cheesy fried eggs were born—three different versions, because variety is the spice of life, don't you know?

15 grams butter

1 egg

15 grams cheddar cheese, grated

Salt and pepper, to taste

FOR METHOD 1: Melt the butter in the pan. Then, crack the egg into the pan, top with cheese, season with salt and pepper, cover, and cook. This should take about 2 minutes on low heat.

FOR METHOD 2: Add the butter and cheddar to a nonstick pan and melt over low heat. Crack the egg over the cheese, season with salt and pepper, and cook until the cheese is fully melted and crispy and the egg is cooked through. Remove and serve.

FOR METHOD 3: Melt the butter in the pan. In a bowl, gently beat the egg just enough to break the yolk but not enough to scramble. Mix in the cheese, season with salt and pepper, and fry until cooked through.

NUTRITION INFO:
(per serving)

CALORIES: 732
NET CARBS: 5 g
CARBS: 10 g

FAT: 58 g
PROTEIN: 33 g
FIBER: 5 g

EGG AND SAUSAGE BREAKFAST SANDWICH

As a one-time die-hard fast-food fan, it was the breakfast items that were the hardest to wean myself off of. There's something about a simple, flavorful, and protein-packed breakfast sandwich that's addicting. If you still get cravings for a McMuffin now and then, here's a sandwich that fills that fast-food void.

200 grams ground pork

½ teaspoon smoked paprika

½ teaspoon dried Italian herbs

Salt and pepper, to taste

1 tablespoon butter, plus more to taste

2 slices American cheese

2 eggs

2 servings Coconut Flour Mug Bread (see 40)

1   In a bowl, mix together the ground pork, smoked paprika, and Italian herbs. Season with salt and pepper.

2   Use a ring mold to shape two hamburger patties from the mixture, or pat them into circles by hand.

3   Heat half of the butter in a frying pan and fry both pork patties over medium heat for about 3 to 4 minutes on each side. Make sure they have a nice crust on the outside and are fully cooked through. Add the slices of cheese to the patties and allow to melt.

4   In the same pan, heat the rest of the butter and use the ring molds to fry the eggs, pricking the yolks after breaking the eggs into the pan.

5   Slice and butter the mug bread and toast them in the same pan.

6   When the bread is toasted, assemble the sandwiches.

SERVINGS: 2
PREP TIME: 5 Minutes
COOKING TIME: 15 Minutes

NUTRITION INFO:
(per serving)

CALORIES: 603
NET CARBS: 2 g
CARBS: 5 g

FAT: 52 g
PROTEIN: 19 g
FIBER: 3 g

EGGS BENEDICT

If there truly was a breakfast fit for a king, it's eggs Benedict. This dish is rich and loaded with calories and fat, and on keto that is a royal way to start the day.

5 grams butter

1 portion 90-Second Mug Bread, cut into 2 slices (see page 35)

2 slices ham

1 teaspoon fresh lemon juice

1 egg yolk

75 grams butter, melted

Salt and pepper, to taste

2 eggs

Fresh chives, for garnish

1 Butter the mug bread and toast on a pan. Then, fry the ham in the same pan.

2 To make the hollandaise, set up a double boiler by placing a bowl over a pot of simmering water.

3 Add the lemon juice and egg yolk into the bowl and mix well. Keep whisking, slowly drizzling in the melted butter until the sauce thickens. Finish by seasoning with salt and pepper.

4 Turn off the stove and leave the bowl over the pot to keep the sauce warm while poaching the eggs.

5 Place another pot of water on the stove and bring it to a simmer. Then, turn down the heat and crack the eggs into the water. After about 3 minutes, remove the eggs with a slotted spoon.

6 Assemble the meal by layering the toasted bread with the ham, then the egg, and pouring the hollandaise over the top. Top with chives and serve.

TIP: In the event that your hollandaise sauce separates, take a warm bowl, add 1 tablespoon of hot water, and slowly whisk it into the broken hollandaise until it comes together again.

NUTRITION INFO:
(per serving)

CALORIES: 516
NET CARBS: 3 g
CARBS: 3 g

FAT: 43 g
PROTEIN: 28 g
FIBER: 0 g

HAM AND MUSHROOM OMELET

As an independent, struggling heavy metal musician, I've always had to do a lot of things myself. One of those was organizing shows, and one of the ways we saved on costs was by having bands stay over at my house. That is how this omelet was born—it became a signature dish that people were willing to travel for. As the bands who stayed over will attest, nothing makes people full (and happy) like this omelet.

3 eggs

Salt, to taste

¼ teaspoon black pepper

½ teaspoon cayenne pepper

½ teaspoon dried oregano

2 tablespoons heavy cream

20 grams Swiss cheese, grated

1 tablespoon butter

1 tablespoon olive oil

20 grams button mushrooms, diced

20 grams ham, cubed

1 Beat the eggs in a bowl with the salt, pepper, cayenne, and oregano. Then, whisk the cream and cheese into the eggs.

2 Heat half the butter and olive oil in the pan. Sauté the mushrooms until they release their water, then add in the chopped ham. Cook until the mixture starts to caramelize.

3 Lower the heat, take the pan off the stove, add the remaining butter and olive oil, and pour in the egg mixture, swirling once. Cover the pan with a lid and cook for 1 to 2 minutes.

4 Fold the mixture over and serve.

NUTRITION INFO:
(per serving)

CALORIES: 430
NET CARBS: 1 g
CARBS: 1 g

FAT: 41 g
PROTEIN: 13 g
FIBER: 0 g

PESTO
SCRAMBLED EGGS

These scrambled eggs were inspired by Dr. Seuss's *Green Eggs and Ham*. The "green" in these creamy eggs comes from basil pesto, which gives them a delicious, herbal note. They're also a hit with kids—just don't forget the ham.

2 eggs

1 tablespoon heavy cream

1 tablespoon Basil Pesto
(see page 22)

1 tablespoon butter

1 Crack the eggs into a bowl and add in the cream and pesto. Beat the mixture with a whisk until the ingredients are well incorporated and the eggs are fluffy.

2 Heat the butter in a nonstick pan, then turn the heat down to the lowest setting and pour in the eggs.

3 Keep moving the eggs around in the pan and let them cook low and slow for about 5 minutes.

4 Once done to your liking, remove and serve.

SERVINGS: 1
PREP TIME: 2 Minutes
COOKING TIME: 5 Minutes

NUTRITION INFO:
(per serving)

CALORIES: 504
NET CARBS: 2 g
CARBS: 3 g

FAT: 40 g
PROTEIN: 31 g
FIBER: 1 g

PIZZA OMELET

I distinctly remember the gas broiler in the old oven at my grandparents' house. My grandfather would make cheese omelets on the stove, finishing them in the oven so the cheese would brown on top. This pizza omelet is in memory of him and his love of good food.

3 eggs

Salt and pepper, to taste

A pinch of cayenne pepper

2 grams fresh parsley, chopped

2 teaspoons olive oil

25 grams pepperoni or salami, sliced

15 grams white mushrooms, sliced

30 grams mozzarella or cheddar cheese, grated

1   Beat the eggs in a bowl with the salt, pepper, cayenne pepper, and parsley.

2   Heat the oil in an oven-safe frying pan and pour in the beaten eggs. Add the toppings, followed by the cheese, and transfer to the oven.

3   Turn on the broiler setting and cook until the cheese on top has melted and the egg is cooked through.

SNACKS AND SIDES

KETO IS PROBABLY HARDEST between four in the afternoon and six in the evening, when lunch is a distant memory and dinner feels a year away. It's the time you reach for a packet of chips or dream of cookies. These snacks and sides work great for those in-between times—if not as an actual precursor to meals—so you aren't tempted to satiate those cravings with carb-filled treats. And they also go well with main courses. These recipes are also great for parties and entertaining—think dips like hummus and baba ghanoush, chicken wings, and fast food favorites like chicken nuggets. No more watching everyone else tuck into hors d'oeuvres while you gnaw on a piece of bacon—with these recipes, everyone's going to want to enjoy what you're eating.

NUTRITION INFO:

(per serving)

CALORIES: 330
NET CARBS: 1 g
CARBS: 1 g

FAT: 22 g
PROTEIN: 30 g
FIBER: 0 g

BACON BOMB
BALLS

The second episode of Headbanger's Kitchen featured the Bacon Bomb (see page 133), a seriously excessive dish for which I was well known in the metal community. At one point, I used to make and sell the Bacon Bomb from home as a way to make a bit of money on the side. It is my signature dish. These Bacon Bomb Balls are a quicker, easier, and simpler version of that recipe, with as much flavor as the original.

250 grams ground pork

5 grams garlic, minced

1 teaspoon fresh rosemary, minced

½ teaspoon five-spice powder

½ teaspoon cayenne pepper

Salt and pepper, to taste

100 grams mozzarella cheese, cubed

250 grams bacon, in long strips

Parmesan cheese, grated, for garnish

Fresh parsley, chopped, for garnish

1 Preheat the oven to 400°F.

2 In a large bowl, combine the pork with the garlic, rosemary, five-spice powder, cayenne pepper, salt, and pepper.

3 Divide the pork mixture into 50-gram portions and shape meatballs around the cubes of mozzarella, essentially making cheese-stuffed meatballs.

4 Wrap each meatball with a slice of bacon and cook in the oven for 20 minutes.

5 Garnish with grated Parmesan cheese and parsley.

SERVINGS: 2
PREP TIME: 1 Hour
COOKING TIME: 30 Minutes

NUTRITION INFO:
(per serving)

CALORIES: 400
NET CARBS: 3 g
CARBS: 3 g

FAT: 22 g
PROTEIN: 49 g
FIBER: 0 g

BACON-WRAPPED CHICKEN

A few years ago, I created a YouTube series called "Bacon Tadka," for which I "baconized" traditional Indian recipes. One recipe I created was tandoori chicken wrapped in bacon. That was an instant hit and inspired this dish. This is a recipe even your kids will love.

2 skinless chicken legs
(drumstick and thigh)

2 tablespoons yogurt

1 tablespoon cream cheese

2 garlic cloves, minced

30 grams mozzarella
or cheddar cheese, grated

Cajun seasoning, to taste

Dried thyme, to taste

Black pepper, to taste

4 strips of bacon

1 Separate the drumstick and thigh and score the chicken pieces with a knife.

2 Mix the yogurt and cream cheese together to form a smooth paste. Microwave the cream cheese for 30 seconds to soften it, if needed.

3 Add the remaining ingredients, except the bacon, to the cream cheese-and-yogurt mixture and then toss the chicken in it. Let it marinate for an hour.

4 Preheat the oven to 410°F.

5 Wrap a strip of bacon around each piece of chicken and bake in the oven for about 20 to 25 minutes, until the chicken is cooked and the bacon crispy. Serve hot.

SERVINGS: 8 (1 serving = 1 nugget)	**NUTRITION INFO:**	**CALORIES:** 58	**FAT:** 3 g
PREP TIME: 25 Minutes	(per serving)	**NET CARBS:** 0 g	**PROTEIN:** 8 g
COOKING TIME: 10 Minutes		**CARBS:** 0 g	**FIBER:** 0 g

CHICKEN NUGGETS

I'm quite vocal about my dislike of fast-food chains, and this recipe takes the guesswork and mystery meat out of the beloved chicken nugget—you're mincing your own so you know exactly what goes into it. And psyllium husk makes a perfect breading, providing some of that crunch we all tend to miss on keto.

250 grams skinless, boneless chicken breast

1 teaspoon Old Bay Seasoning

Salt and pepper, to taste

1 egg

Psyllium husk, as needed

Lard or any fat of choice, for frying

1   In a food processor, blend chicken, Old Bay Seasoning, salt, and pepper to get a nice, fine chicken mince, almost like a paste.

2   With wet hands, shape the chicken mince into nugget-like shapes and refrigerate for about 15 minutes.

3   Beat the egg lightly with some salt.

4   Dip a nugget in the egg first, then coat with the husk; repeat until all the nuggets are coated.

5   Deep fry in cooking fat of choice; cooking time is approximately 4 minutes.

6   Once cooked, drain off excessive oil and then serve with Tomato Ketchup (see page 26) or Barbeque Sauce (see page 21).

SERVINGS: 5 (1 serving = 2 pot-stickers)
PREP TIME: 15 Minutes
COOKING TIME: 25 Minutes

NUTRITION INFO FOR POT STICKERS:
(per serving)

CALORIES: 157 **FAT:** 7 g
NET CARBS: 3 g **PROTEIN:** 21 g
CARBS: 4 g **FIBER:** 1 g

NUTRITION INFO FOR DIPPING SAUCE:
(per serving; this recipe makes 2 servings)

CALORIES: 43 **FAT:** 4 g
NET CARBS: 2 g **PROTEIN:** 1 g
CARBS: 2 g **FIBER:** 0 g

CHICKEN POT-STICKERS

Every country seems to have its version of a dumpling. Both the craving for these and the inspiration for them hit at the same time. I thought, why not try cabbage as the outer skin? Only later did I find out that this dish is very similar to Polish cabbage rolls, or golbaki. Either way, it's delicious and can be customized to your taste, be it with a meat or vegetable filling.

For the Dipping Sauce

1 teaspoon peanut butter (natural and with no sugar added)

1 teaspoon Sriracha

1 teaspoon olive oil

½ teaspoon soy sauce

½ teaspoon rice wine vinegar

Juice of ½ a lime

Salt, to taste

½ teaspoon ginger-garlic paste

For the Chicken Pot-Stickers

1 cabbage

500 grams ground chicken

25 grams onion, grated

1 teaspoon ginger-garlic paste

½ spring onion, chopped

5 grams fresh cilantro, chopped

1 tablespoon sesame oil

Salt and pepper, to taste

1 To make the dipping sauce, combine all the ingredients in a bowl and stir together.

2 In a large pot, boil a whole cabbage in water for 8 to 10 minutes and then, once cooled, peel off 10 full leaves.

3 In a large bowl, mix together the rest of the pot-sticker ingredients.

4 Using a spoon, scoop out a portion of the meat mixture (about 50 grams) and place in a boiled cabbage leaf. Wrap the meat tightly in the leaf to create a dumpling.

5 Steam the parcels for about 10 minutes and then place in a frying pan for another 2 to 3 minutes, frying on each side until golden brown.

6 Serve the dumplings with the dipping sauce.

SERVINGS: 15 (1 serving = 1 full wing)
PREP TIME: 15 Minutes
COOKING TIME: 25 Minutes

NUTRITION INFO:
(per serving)

CALORIES: 166
NET CARBS: 0 g
CARBS: 0 g

FAT: 9 g
PROTEIN: 20 g
FIBER: 0 g

BUFFALO WINGS

The first time I ate a Buffalo wing was when the Hard Rock Cafe opened in Mumbai, over a decade ago. And it was quite the revelation—the tangy sauce, the crisp wings, that cooling blue cheese dip. It quickly became a staple order every time I played there or went for a show. Sadly, the quality of the wings took a nosedive over the years and I stopped eating them altogether. I'd forgotten all about them, actually, until my friend Joe Duff of Duff's Famous Wings sent over two bottles of his family's secret recipe Buffalo wings sauce. Of course, a keto version had to happen, and, in my humble opinion, these are far better than what the Hard Rock Cafe ever made.

1 teaspoon salt

1 teaspoon black pepper

1 teaspoon paprika

100 ml hot sauce of choice

1 kg chicken wings, separated into drumette and flat

50 grams butter

25 grams cream cheese

Celery sticks, for serving

Blue cheese or dip of choice, for serving

1. Preheat the oven to 400°F. In a large bowl combine salt, pepper, paprika, and 50 ml of hot sauce and marinate the chicken wings for about 10 minutes.

2. Layer the wings on a wire rack in a baking sheet and cook for about 25 minutes.

3. Heat the butter and cream cheese in the microwave for about 30 seconds or until the butter is completely melted. Add the remaining 50 ml of the hot sauce into the melted butter and cheese and give it all a good mix.

4. Once the wings are cooked, toss them in the melted butter sauce.

5. Serve the wings with some celery sticks and dip of choice.

SERVINGS: 9 (1 serving = 1 full wing)
PREP TIME: 10 Minutes
COOKING TIME: 35 Minutes

NUTRITION INFO:

(per serving)

CALORIES: 263

NET CARBS: 1 g

CARBS: 1 g

FAT: 12 g

PROTEIN: 35 g

FIBER: 0 g

GARLIC-PARMESAN CHICKEN WINGS

My very first chicken wing recipe was also my most popular. The secret to the crispiness is the double-baking. I always recommend that people use good Parmesan cheese to make these, because it makes a huge difference to the flavor.

9 full chicken wings, separated into drumette and flat

1 teaspoon salt

½ teaspoon pepper

½ teaspoon cayenne pepper

1 teaspoon smoked paprika

1 teaspoon dried oregano

1 tablespoon butter, melted

1 teaspoon fresh lemon juice

1 tablespoon hot sauce

10 grams garlic, minced

1 teaspoon fresh parsley, chopped

50 grams Parmesan cheese, grated

1 Preheat oven to 375°F.

2 Season the wings with salt, pepper, cayenne, paprika, oregano, butter, and lemon juice.

3 Bake wings for 20 to 25 minutes.

4 Remove the wings and increase the oven temperature to 400°F.

5 Toss the wings in hot sauce, garlic, parsley, and Parmesan cheese and return to the oven, baking for an additional 10 minutes.

6 Remove from the oven and serve immediately.

SERVINGS: 7 (1 serving = 1 full wing)
PREP TIME: 1 Hour
COOKING TIME: 25 Minutes

NUTRITION INFO:
(per serving)

CALORIES: 103
NET CARBS: 2 g
CARBS: 2 g

FAT: 5 g
PROTEIN: 11 g
FIBER: 0 g

PEANUT SAUCE CHICKEN WINGS

I love the versatility of chicken wings. When it comes to Asian flavors, playing around with peanut butter reminds me of chicken satay, which is the inspiration behind these wings.

16 grams peanut butter
(natural and with no sugar added)

30 ml coconut cream or coconut milk

10 ml soy sauce

15 ml rice vinegar

10 ml Sriracha

10 ml fish sauce

Salt and pepper, to taste

½ teaspoon ginger powder

½ teaspoon garlic powder

500 grams chicken wings
(approximately 7 full wings),
separated into drumette and flat

¼ teaspoon black sesame seeds

¼ teaspoon white sesame seeds

Keto-friendly hot sauce, for serving

1 Mix the peanut butter, coconut milk, soy sauce, vinegar, Sriracha, fish sauce, salt, pepper, ginger, and garlic powder in a bowl. Then, add in the chicken wings and mix until evenly coated.

2 Allow the chicken wings to marinate for at least an hour, or even overnight in the fridge. Then, sprinkle with the sesame seeds.

3 Preheat the oven to 410°F. Once to temperature, bake the chicken wings on a wire rack in a baking sheet for about 25 to 30 minutes, until they're cooked through.

4 Serve your favorite keto-friendly hot sauce.

SERVINGS: 2
PREP TIME: 5 Minutes
COOKING TIME: 5 Minutes

NUTRITION INFO:
(per serving)

CALORIES: 271
NET CARBS: 7 g
CARBS: 7 g

FAT: 22 g
PROTEIN: 21 g
FIBER: 0 g

BUTTER AND GARLIC CALAMARI

If you've ever found yourself on the sunny beaches of Goa, you've probably been served a plate of this. You smell it before you see it—garlic roasted in butter, then a whiff of the sea. My mouth is watering just thinking about it. The Goan iteration is loaded with garlic but mine is more mellow and allows the tender squid to shine through. It's quick to whip up and easier still to love, and the results are always impressive.

250 grams calamari rings

Salt and pepper, to taste

50 grams salted butter

20 grams garlic, minced

3 grams fresh parsley, chopped

3 grams fresh cilantro, chopped

5 grams spring onion, chopped, greens reserved for garnish

5 grams Parmesan cheese, grated

A squeeze of fresh lemon juice

1   Season the squid with salt and pepper and set aside.

2   In a frying pan, heat butter. When it starts to foam, add in the garlic, parsley, cilantro, and spring onion and cook over medium heat until the garlic starts to brown.

3   Turn the heat up to high and add calamari, stirring frequently for 2 to 3 minutes, until the squid is just fully cooked through.

4   Mix in Parmesan cheese, check seasoning, and add lemon juice.

5   Plate and garnish with spring onion greens.

TIP: Squid cooks very quickly, so if there is a lot of liquid in the pan, remove the squid, cook down the liquid and, once it's almost gone, add the squid back, then turn off the heat and finish the dish.

SERVINGS: 6 (1 serving = 1 fish cake)
PREP TIME: 5 Minutes
COOKING TIME: 20 Minutes

NUTRITION INFO:
(per serving)

CALORIES: 149
NET CARBS: 1 g
CARBS: 1 g

FAT: 9 g
PROTEIN: 15 g
FIBER: 0 g

FISH CAKES

Fish cakes are called fish tikki in India, where "tikki" is any kind of small cutlet or croquette of minced meat or veggies. Usually it's a great way to use up odds and ends of cooked fish, like parts of the head or meat around the tail, but it can also be made from canned tuna or salmon. These make great appetizers and also work as a quick snack. In fact, you could team this with some 90-Second Mug Bread (see page 35) to make a fish burger.

240 grams canned tuna or salmon

30 grams red onion, diced

A few sprigs of fresh parsley, chopped

1 tablespoon mayonnaise

1 teaspoon mustard

1 teaspoon hot sauce

½ teaspoon garlic powder

½ teaspoon paprika

50 grams Bread Crumbs (see page 25)

Salt and pepper, to taste

2 eggs

1 tablespoon butter

1 Open the can of fish and drain the liquid, then add the fish to a large mixing bowl.

2 Fold in the onion, parsley, mayonnaise, mustard, hot sauce, garlic powder, paprika, Bread Crumbs, salt, and pepper.

3 Add the eggs and give it all a good mix.

4 Use a cookie cutter or ring mold to shape the fish cakes or shape them by hand.

5 Heat butter in a nonstick skillet and fry the fish cakes over medium heat for about 3 to 4 minutes per side.

6 Once done, remove from the pan and serve hot.

SERVINGS: 1
PREP TIME: 35 Minutes
COOKING TIME: 5 Minutes

NUTRITION INFO:
(per serving)

CALORIES: 452
NET CARBS: 3 g
CARBS: 5 g

FAT: 39 g
PROTEIN: 23 g
FIBER: 2 g

GARLIC BUTTER PRAWNS

Could there be a more delectable combination than garlic and butter? These prawns are another staple menu item that you'll find in almost every seafood restaurant in Mumbai. This one will leave you licking the plate clean.

100 grams prawns
¼ teaspoon salt
¼ teaspoon pepper
¼ teaspoon cayenne pepper
½ teaspoon dried oregano
1 tablespoon olive oil
2 tablespoons butter
5 grams garlic, minced
5 grams fresh parsley, chopped
Juice of ½ lemon

1   Toss the prawns with the salt, pepper, cayenne, and oregano and leave to marinate in the refrigerator for about 30 minutes.

2   Heat olive oil and 1 tablespoon butter in frying pan. Once the butter froths, add in the garlic followed by the parsley. Next, add in the prawns and cook until opaque, about 4 minutes.

3   Turn off the heat and add the rest of the butter and the lemon juice.

4   Stir until the butter melts and serve.

TIP: Prawns cook very quickly, so if they release a lot of liquid into the pan, take them out, cook to reduce the liquid, then throw the prawns back in once the liquid is almost gone.

NUTRITION INFO:
(per serving)

CALORIES: 95
NET CARBS: 4 g
CARBS: 6 g

FAT: 7 g
PROTEIN: 2 g
FIBER: 2 g

BABA GHANOUSH

I hated eggplant as a kid. There was something about its slimy texture and those strange seeds that just didn't appeal to me. But when I hit my late 20s, my tastes did a 180-degree flip. I really grew to appreciate eggplant's meaty texture, which tastes best when it's roasted over an open flame until the skin is blistered and the flesh is soft enough to scoop out. Throw in some lemon juice and tahini and the smoky flavor of the eggplant is amplified, making the perfect dip for keto crackers.

500 grams eggplant
2 cloves of garlic, diced
50 grams tahini
½ teaspoon fresh lemon juice
1 teaspoon salt
½ teaspoon cumin powder
½ teaspoon paprika
¼ teaspoon cayenne pepper
2 tablespoons olive oil
1 tablespoon fresh parsley, chopped, for garnish

1 Pierce the skin of a large eggplant and roast over an open flame or in the oven for 15 to 20 minutes at 400°F.

2 Once roasted, allow it to cool and then peel off the skin. Don't worry if a few bits of charred skin remain. Alternatively, cut the eggplant in half lengthwise and scoop out the flesh with a spoon.

3 Roughly chop the roasted eggplant and mix with the garlic, tahini, lemon juice, seasonings, and half the olive oil.

4 Drizzle the remaining olive oil on top and garnish with chopped parsley before serving.

TIP: For a creamier texture, use a food processor to blend the eggplant; for a chunkier preparation, chop with a knife.

SERVINGS: 12

PREP TIME: 5 Minutes

COOKING TIME: 10 Minutes

NUTRITION INFO:

(per serving)

CALORIES: 150

NET CARBS: 3 g

CARBS: 5 g

FAT: 14 g

PROTEIN: 2 g

FIBER: 2 g

CAULIFLOWER HUMMUS

Apart from being the new potato and the new rice, cauliflower is also the new chickpea—softened, boiled cauliflower, when pureed, makes a rich and creamy hummus. This is so close to the real thing, you'll be surprised.

500 grams cauliflower, cut, florets separated

60 grams tahini

10 grams garlic

8 tablespoons extra virgin olive oil

100 grams Kalamata olives

1 teaspoon paprika

1 teaspoon cumin

Juice of 1 lemon

Salt and pepper, to taste

1 tablespoon fresh parsley, chopped, plus more for garnish

Olives, for garnish

1   Microwave the cauliflower for 10 minutes, until tender. The cauliflower can also be steamed or boiled until tender.

2   In a food processor combine all ingredients, except the garnishes, and blitz until the mixture is nice and smooth.

3   Taste and adjust the seasoning if necessary.

4   Transfer to a bowl and garnish with additional parsley, and olives for luck.

SERVINGS: 4
PREP TIME: 5 Minutes
COOKING TIME: 10 Minutes

NUTRITION INFO:
(per serving)

CALORIES: 162
NET CARBS: 3 g
CARBS: 6 g

FAT: 15 g
PROTEIN: 3 g
FIBER: 3 g

CAULIFLOWER MASH

If I ever get a tattoo, it'll say "cauliflower is the new potato," because that discovery is the foundation of keto. I never appreciated how versatile this vegetable was before, and now here we are, turning it into everything from hummus to pizza. Even the potato can't perform in some of those arenas. Here, cauliflower takes the form of a creamy mash, so perfect in texture and taste, you'll never guess it's not a potato.

450 grams cauliflower, separated into large florets

50 grams butter

50 ml heavy cream

Salt and pepper, to taste

1   Boil the cauliflower in salted water for about 10 minutes or until tender. Once cooked, the cauliflower should be easy to slice.

2   Add the boiled cauliflower, butter, cream, salt, and pepper to a food processor and blitz until it is a rich, smooth paste. Serve immediately.

TIP: Since the consistency of cream varies across the world, add in a little at a time so that you get the thickness you like.

SERVINGS: 2
PREP TIME: 5 Minutes
COOKING TIME: 10 Minutes

NUTRITION INFO:
(per serving)

CALORIES: 328
NET CARBS: 3 g
CARBS: 5 g

FAT: 29 g
PROTEIN: 14 g
FIBER: 2 g

CHEESY BACON SLAW

I've always made coleslaw with mayo and raw cabbage, usually as part of my tuna salad, but warm slaw makes a great side dish on its own, and is a fantastic way to sneak some vegetables and fiber into your diet. And do you honestly need an excuse to eat bacon, cabbage, and cheese?

100 grams bacon, chopped

150 grams cabbage, grated

Salt and pepper, to taste

¼ teaspoon paprika

½ teaspoon dried oregano

30 grams cheddar cheese, grated

50 ml heavy cream

Fresh parsley, chopped, for garnish

1   In a cold pan, fry the bacon over medium heat and allow the fat to render.

2   Once the bacon is cooked to your liking, add in the cabbage and season with the salt, pepper, paprika, and dried oregano. As the cabbage starts to soften, add in the cheese and cream and mix well.

3   Once the cabbage is cooked to your liking, turn off the heat, garnish with fresh parsley, and serve.

SERVINGS: 1
PREP TIME: 2 Minutes
COOKING TIME: 5 Minutes

NUTRITION INFO:
(per serving)

CALORIES: 283
NET CARBS: 2 g
CARBS: 4 g

FAT: 26 g
PROTEIN: 9 g
FIBER: 2 g

CREAMED SPINACH

I discovered creamed spinach rather late in life. I wasn't a huge fan of spinach growing up, and it wasn't a staple at my house or on restaurant menus. This creamed spinach recipe, however, changed the game. Perfect on the side with a well-seared steak or a piece of roast chicken, it's another great way to get your greens.

1 tablespoon olive oil
100 grams spinach
Salt and pepper, to taste
⅛ teaspoon nutmeg
10 grams butter
20 grams Parmesan cheese, grated
30 ml heavy cream

1   Heat the olive oil in a pan, then add the spinach. Season with salt, pepper, and nutmeg and cook until wilted.

2   Once the spinach wilts, add the butter, cheese, and cream and cook for 1 minute before serving.

SERVINGS: 1
PREP TIME: 5 Minutes
COOKING TIME: 5 Minutes

NUTRITION INFO:
(per serving)

CALORIES: 250
NET CARBS: 5 g
CARBS: 7 g

FAT: 22 g
PROTEIN: 10 g
FIBER: 2 g

SAUTÉED MUSHROOMS

I love mushrooms. I'm only just discovering the sheer variety of textures and flavors they come in. They're packed with nutrition and punch up any dish they're in. I've been making these mushrooms for years now, and including them in this book was a no-brainer. Feel free to use any mushrooms you like. My original recipe had a splash of vodka in it as well, which you could add in if you're feeling naughty. These used to sit on top of my beef burgers as a condiment, but now they are my go-to snack or an accompaniment to breakfast, lunch, and dinner. Ain't no time like mushroom time.

1 tablespoon olive or coconut oil

100 grams white button mushrooms, sliced

50 grams oyster mushrooms, roughly chopped

Salt and pepper, to taste

1 tablespoon butter

1 sprig fresh rosemary

1 garlic clove, minced

1   Heat the oil in the pan until it's near smoking. Then, add in the mushrooms and season with salt and pepper. Add half the butter and rosemary and cook until the mushrooms release their liquid.

2   Add in the garlic and fry until it starts to brown. Then, turn the stove off and add in the remaining butter. Stir until it melts and serve immediately.

SOUPS AND SALADS

BECAUSE OF MY SMALL APPETITE, I wasn't always the biggest fan of soups; I saw them as something that got in the way of eating "real food," since most soups in India are cornstarch-thickened monstrosities that fill you with empty calories. But these soups are complete meals in themselves, and same goes for the salads. On keto, soups and salads are a great way to get your daily veggies in and balance out your fat macros, as well as get great flavor in a snap. Soups are ideal make-ahead meals because they scale well, are easy to make in big batches, and are the quickest thing to reheat on a busy weeknight.

SERVINGS: 4
PREP TIME: 10 Minutes
COOKING TIME: 25 Minutes

NUTRITION INFO:
(per serving)

CALORIES: 356
NET CARBS: 8 g
CARBS: 12 g

FAT: 30 g
PROTEIN: 10 g
FIBER: 4 g

CHEESE AND BROCCOLI SOUP

I don't think I know of any other soup that combines cheese and veggies so deliciously. This remains one of the most popular recipes on my channel and it's easy to see why. After all, who can resist spoonable, drinkable cheese?

1 tablespoon olive oil

3 tablespoons butter

50 grams onion, roughly chopped

500 grams broccoli, stalks roughly chopped, florets diced

10 grams garlic, minced

Salt, to taste

½ teaspoon pepper

1 teaspoon paprika

½ teaspoon cayenne pepper

500 ml chicken or vegetable stock, or water

150 ml heavy cream

100 grams cheddar cheese, grated

1   Heat up 1 tablespoon of olive oil and 1 tablespoon of butter in a saucepan. Once hot, add in the onion and the broccoli stalks. Cook over medium heat until the onion starts to brown, then add in the garlic.

2   Once the veggies start to color, season with salt, pepper, paprika and cayenne pepper and cook out the spices for a minute. Deglaze with chicken or vegetable stock, or water, then cover and cook for 5 minutes.

3   Transfer the contents of the saucepan to a food processor and blend with the liquid until you get a smooth and creamy soup.

4   In the same pan, heat the remaining butter and fry the broccoli florets, without stirring, for a seared outside.

5   Pour the blended soup mixture through a sieve into the pot. For a chunkier soup, do not strain the soup.

6   Allow the mixture to come to a boil, then simmer for a few minutes. Add in the heavy cream and cheese and mix well.

7   Cook until all the cheese melts. If desired, blend the soup further. Serve hot.

SERVINGS: 4
PREP TIME: 10 Minutes
COOKING TIME: 25 Minutes

NUTRITION INFO:
(per serving)

CALORIES: 259
NET CARBS: 3 g
CARBS: 3 g

FAT: 20 g
PROTEIN: 1 g
FIBER: 0 g

CREAM OF CHICKEN SOUP

What is usually a bland soup made with stock and cream becomes a flavorful comfort food in this recipe. The additional vegetables and seasonings take this soup to the next level and create a winter weather keto staple. You won't even notice that the traditional roux has disappeared.

200 grams boneless chicken, chopped

Salt, to taste

½ teaspoon pepper

½ teaspoon dried oregano

¼ teaspoon cayenne pepper

45 grams butter

1 tablespoon olive oil

1 spring onion, whites and greens separated, chopped

20 grams celery, chopped

3 garlic cloves, minced

500 ml chicken stock

200 ml water

100 ml heavy cream

10 grams celery leaves or fresh parsley, chopped

1 Season the chicken with salt, pepper, dried oregano, and cayenne pepper.

2 Melt the butter in the saucepan with the olive oil, then add the spring onion whites and the celery and fry.

3 Add in the chicken pieces and cook over high heat. Then, add the garlic and spring onion greens and cook until the garlic starts to brown.

4 Add in the chicken stock and water, check the seasoning, and bring to a gentle boil.

5 Turn off the heat and add the cream and celery leaves or parsley. For a thicker soup, continue to cook after adding the cream until the soup has reduced to the desired consistency. Serve warm.

NUTRITION INFO:
(per serving)

CALORIES: 230
NET CARBS: 6 g
CARBS: 8 g

FAT: 21 g
PROTEIN: 4 g
FIBER: 2 g

CREAM OF MUSHROOM SOUP

You'll find cans of this soup on the dustiest store shelves in India. To avoid the bland taste of that canned staple, I used a mix of mushrooms and pureed them to get a nice, thick consistency. While you'll definitely want to go for a second bowl, you won't find yourself reaching for another canned soup after this.

2 tablespoons olive oil

3 tablespoons butter

10 grams garlic, minced

125 grams button mushrooms, stalks chopped, caps sliced

125 grams portobello mushrooms, stalks chopped, caps sliced

1 chicken or vegetable bouillon cube

½ teaspoon salt

½ teaspoon pepper

¼ teaspoon cayenne pepper

½ teaspoon paprika

300 ml water

100 ml cream

100 grams oyster mushrooms, roughly chopped

1 teaspoon Parmesan cheese per serving, for garnish

Fresh basil, chopped, for garnish

1. In a large saucepan, heat 1 tablespoon of olive oil and 1 tablespoon butter and fry the garlic.

2. Once the garlic starts to brown, add the mushroom stalks and a handful of the sliced mushroom caps. Season with the bouillon cube, and half the salt, pepper, cayenne, and all the paprika and mix well.

3. Once the mushrooms release their liquid, add the water and cook for 2 minutes. Then, transfer mixture to a blender and blend until smooth.

4. In the same pan, heat 1 tablespoon of butter and fry the remaining sliced mushrooms. Once they release their water, strain the blended soup mixture into the pan with a fine sieve.

5. Bring the mixture to a simmer. Once the mushrooms are cooked through, add the cream and turn off the stove or continue cooking and reduce to the desired consistency.

6. Add the oyster mushrooms to a frying pan with the remaining butter, olive oil, salt, pepper, and cayenne and fry until crispy.

7. Garnish with cheese, fried oyster mushrooms, and fresh basil and serve.

SERVINGS: 2
PREP TIME: 5 Minutes
COOKING TIME: 15 Minutes

NUTRITION INFO:
(per serving)

CALORIES: 216
NET CARBS: 7 g
CARBS: 9 g

FAT: 19 g
PROTEIN: 4 g
FIBER: 2g

SPINACH SOUP

I never liked spinach as a child, but somewhere along the way I discovered a love for it, particularly in soup. This creamy and rich soup became a quick favorite of mine and is the best way to get in your greens on keto.

1 tablespoon butter

50 grams onion, roughly chopped

10 grams garlic, roughly chopped

150 grams spinach

1 chicken bouillon cube

300 ml water

100 ml heavy cream

Pepper, to taste

1 Melt the butter in a saucepan and sauté the onion until translucent. Add in the garlic and cook until it starts to brown.

2 Next, add the spinach, bouillon cube, and half the water. Cover and cook until the spinach wilts. Mix, then transfer into a blender or use an immersion blender to puree until the soup becomes smooth.

3 Run through a fine sieve and add water depending on how thick you like the soup, then bring to gentle simmer and add the cream.

4 Reduce the liquid down to your desired thickness, then top with pepper before serving.

NUTRITION INFO:
(per serving)

CALORIES: 266
NET CARBS: 5 g
CARBS: 7 g

FAT: 26 g
PROTEIN: 2 g
FIBER: 2 g

TOMATO SOUP

This light, comforting soup will warm you right through with festive feelings thanks to the pumpkin spice. In India, this has become my rainy-day staple, but it's perfect no matter what the weather decides to throw at you.

50 grams salted butter

50 grams onion, chopped

Salt, to taste

10 grams garlic, chopped

300 grams tomatoes, canned or fresh, chopped

Water, as needed

½ teaspoon black pepper powder

½ teaspoon smoked paprika

1 teaspoon pumpkin spice

100 ml chicken stock, plus more as needed

100 ml heavy cream

Freshly cracked pepper, for garnish

Fresh basil, chopped, for garnish

Parmesan cheese, grated, for garnish

1 Heat the butter in a heavy bottomed saucepan, then add the onion and salt. Cook the onion on low until it starts to turn brown and caramelize.

2 Add in the garlic and cook until it starts to brown, then add the tomatoes and cook for about 2 minutes. Cover and cook over low heat for 5 minutes. If the mix looks too dry, add some water to prevent it from burning.

3 After 5 minutes of cooking, add in the black pepper powder, paprika, pumpkin spice, and chicken stock. Cover with a lid and cook for about 10 minutes, stirring every few minutes, until the tomatoes are completely soft. Let cool.

4 Next, puree the mixture in a food processor or using an immersion blender. Add more stock if needed to make it easier to blend.

5 Strain the liquid for a smoother soup, or add more stock if the soup is too thick. Add the heavy cream and heat through.

6 Garnish with fresh pepper, basil, and cheese and serve.

SERVINGS: 2	NUTRITION INFO:	CALORIES: 601	FAT: 45 g
PREP TIME: 5 Minutes	(per serving)	NET CARBS: 5 g	PROTEIN: 43 g
COOKING TIME: 15 Minutes		CARBS: 8 g	FIBER: 3 g

ASIAN BEEF SALAD

I created this recipe as part of a "salad week" series I ran on my YouTube channel, and since I'd already done two chicken salads, I wanted to do something with beef. Fortunately, the Asian-inspired, peanut-based dressing paired beautifully with it. I used enoki mushrooms here because they create a noodle-like texture, but you can work with any mushroom you like.

For the Peanut-Soy Dressing

2 tablespoons olive oil

1 tablespoon peanut butter (natural and with no sugar added)

1 garlic clove, minced

1 teaspoon low-carb soy sauce

1 teaspoon white vinegar

1 squirt fish sauce

1 squeeze fresh lime juice

2 drops stevia

Salt and pepper, to taste

For the Salad

300 grams filet steak or cut of choice, sliced into thin strips

Salt, to taste

Curry powder, to taste

1 tablespoon olive oil, for frying

1 tablespoon butter

100 grams enoki mushrooms or mushroom of choice, chopped

100 grams mixed lettuce

Fresh cilantro, chopped, for garnish

1 teaspoon sesame seeds, for garnish

1. For the dressing, place all the ingredients in a bowl and whisk together to emulsify.

2. Season the beef strips with salt and curry powder. Heat the olive oil in a frying pan. When it is very hot, add the beef, fry until cooked to preference, and set aside.

3. In the same pan, add the butter, mushrooms, and salt to the beef drippings and stir-fry until the liquid evaporates.

4. Assemble the salad with the lettuce, beef, mushrooms, and dressing, and top with cilantro and sesame seeds.

SERVINGS: 2	NUTRITION INFO:	CALORIES: 442	FAT: 35 g
PREP TIME: 40 Minutes	(per serving)	NET CARBS: 5 g	PROTEIN: 27 g
COOKING TIME: 10 Minutes		CARBS: 6 g	FIBER: 1 g

CHICKEN SALAD

When people think of a keto-friendly salad, they think of something drowning in cream and fat. I wanted to create a salad that was high in calories, with a good amount of fat, but at the same time didn't coat the inside of your mouth with grease. This salad is refreshing with a creamy yogurt-based dressing that helps you hit your fat macros but doesn't feel as heavy and oily as mayo-based dressings would.

For the Salad

175 grams boneless chicken leg and thigh meat

Salt, to taste

½ teaspoon pepper

1 teaspoon dried herb seasoning mix

½ tablespoon apple cider vinegar

½ tablespoon olive oil

½ tablespoon bacon fat, olive oil, coconut oil, butter, or ghee, for frying

½ tablespoon butter

100 grams lettuce, sliced

50 grams tomato, sliced

100 grams cucumber, sliced

30 grams olives, sliced

50 grams feta cheese, crumbled

For the Dressing

1 tablespoon full-fat Greek yogurt

2 tablespoons olive oil

1 teaspoon fresh lime or lemon juice

Resting juices from the chicken

Salt and pepper, to taste

½ teaspoon cayenne pepper

1 Marinate the chicken with salt, pepper, dried herbs, apple cider vinegar, and olive oil, for at least 30 minutes.

2 Heat the frying oil in a pan and add the chicken. Cook the chicken for 2 to 3 minutes per side. Add the butter to the pan and baste the chicken repeatedly with the melted butter.

3 Once cooked, remove the chicken and set aside. Make sure you pour all the residual fat from the pan onto the chicken as well. Once the chicken has rested, pour out all the resting juices and set aside.

4 In a mixing bowl, take the yogurt, olive oil, lime or lemon juice, and resting juices and mix. Season with salt, pepper, and cayenne. This is the dressing.

5 Place the vegetables into a bowl. Then, slice the chicken and add to the bowl. Crumble in the feta cheese and top with the dressing.

SERVINGS: 2
PREP TIME: 20 Minutes
COOKING TIME: 10 Minutes

NUTRITION INFO:
(per serving)

CALORIES: 409
NET CARBS: 2 g
CARBS: 3 g

FAT: 32 g
PROTEIN: 28 g
FIBER: 1 g

PESTO CHICKEN SALAD

This recipe was inspired by a trip to Italy in 2013 with my then-girlfriend-now-wife. For our very first meal in Rome, we ate a caprese salad and I instantly fell in love with the holy trifecta of mozzarella, basil, and tomato. I tried to recreate that feeling with this recipe, taking a basic chicken salad up a notch with mozzarella and a delicious pesto.

For the Salad

150 grams boneless chicken leg and thigh meat

1 teaspoon Italian seasoning

Salt, to taste

1 teaspoon olive oil

15 grams pine nuts

1 tablespoon bacon fat, for frying

100 grams mixed lettuce

50 grams cherry tomatoes

100 grams bocconcini
(small mozzarella cheese balls)

For the Dressing

1 tablespoon Basil Pesto
(see page 22)

2 tablespoons mayonnaise

Resting juices from the chicken

1 Season the chicken with the Italian seasoning, salt, and olive oil and let marinate for about 10 minutes.

2 Toast the pine nuts in a dry pan and set aside once they turn brown.

3 Heat the bacon fat in the same pan and once hot, fry the chicken, cooking for about 3 to 4 minutes per side. Set aside.

4 Mix all the ingredients for the dressing and set aside.

5 Slice the chicken into strips and the cherry tomatoes into halves, then place them in a bowl with the pine nuts and bocconcini. Top with the dressing and serve.

SERVINGS: 1	**NUTRITION INFO:**	**CALORIES:** 574	**FAT:** 42 g
PREP TIME: 10 Minutes	(per serving)	**NET CARBS:** 7 g	**PROTEIN:** 38 g
COOKING TIME: 10 Minutes		**CARBS:** 9 g	**FIBER:** 2 g

SEAFOOD SALAD

This is my attempt to refashion shrimp cocktail into something you'd actually want to eat. I'm not always the biggest seafood lover, but seafood works incredibly well in cold salads, and the butter-poached prawns, soft-boiled eggs, and lettuce create a salad that you won't want to miss.

25 grams red onion, sliced

A few drops of fresh lemon juice

30 grams salted butter

2 whole garlic cloves

Salt and pepper, to taste

10 grams mixed dried herbs

150 grams prawns

15 grams mayonnaise

8 grams Sriracha

Fresh dill, to taste

100 grams mixed lettuce

30 grams black olives, chopped

30 grams gherkins, chopped

1 soft-boiled egg, halved

1 Mix the red onion with the lemon juice and set aside to pickle.

2 Melt the butter in a saucepan on the lowest heat, add the garlic, salt, pepper, and dried herbs. Once the butter starts bubbling, add the prawns and cook slowly.

3 Once the prawns are cooked through, remove the prawns and garlic with a slotted spoon and grate the garlic into a bowl.

4 Add in the mayonnaise, Sriracha, and the butter that was used to cook the prawns to the bowl and mix well. Finish with the fresh dill.

5 Place the pickled onion, lettuce, black olives, gherkins, and soft-boiled egg in a bowl and toss to distribute. Top with the prawn-and-garlic dressing, toss to combine, and serve.

SERVINGS: 4
PREP TIME: 5 Minutes
COOKING TIME: 10 Minutes

NUTRITION INFO:
(per serving)

CALORIES: 326
NET CARBS: 0 g
CARBS: 6 g

FAT: 25 g
PROTEIN: 22 g
FIBER: 6 g

TUNA SALAD

Tuna is not exactly indigenous to India. We always had visiting relatives bring us little cans of tuna from other countries when I was growing up, so my mother concocted a truly spectacular salad recipe with it. Mine is true to hers with one little twist—bacon. After all, what salad is complete without it?

4 eggs

100 grams cabbage, julienned

4 tablespoons mayonnaise

2 tablespoons horseradish sauce

2 strips bacon, cooked and chopped

Salt and pepper, to taste

200 grams canned tuna, drained

20 grams celery, diced

20 grams spring onion, diced

20 grams lettuce, diced

20 grams green bell pepper, diced

1 teaspoon mustard

1 teaspoon Sriracha

1. Boil the eggs for about 6 minutes and let cool. Once cool, peel and set aside.

2. Mix the cabbage with 2 tablespoons mayonnaise, 1 tablespoon horseradish sauce, and the bacon. Season with salt and pepper, mix well, and set aside.

3. Roughly chop two of the eggs, then break the tuna with a fork and add to the eggs. Mix well.

4. Add in the celery, spring onion, lettuce, bell pepper, remaining mayonnaise and horseradish sauce, 1 teaspoon mustard, Sriracha, season with salt and pepper, and mix well.

5. Combine the cabbage mix and tuna mix. Cut the remaining eggs in half, place them on top of the salad, and serve.

MAIN COURSES

HERE IS THE MEAT AND POTATOES of this book (pun intended). I've always been a savory cook, and these meaty mains are testament to that. Of course, I haven't forgotten my vegetarian friends; I've included some of my favorite strictly veggie dishes that would win over even the most hardcore carnivores. You'll find no exotic ingredients here, no unpronounceable chemical compounds, no molecular gastronomy—the idea here is to take the intimidation out of keto cooking and simplify the process so even a newbie who's never boiled an egg can make a wholesome meal out of kitchen staples. A lot of these recipes are one-pot, and there are even one-person meals for those going the keto mile alone. There's just one simple rule to these—remember to always taste as you go along and cook by intuition. It's how I've learned, and I promise it'll make you a better cook. Bon appétit!

SERVINGS: 5
PREP TIME: 40 Minutes
COOKING TIME: 45 Minutes

NUTRITION INFO:
(per serving)

CALORIES: 435
NET CARBS: 1 g
CARBS: 1 g

FAT: 36 g
PROTEIN: 26 g
FIBER: 0 g

BACON BOMB

This was the dish that laid the foundation for Headbanger's Kitchen: a pork meatloaf stuffed with cheese and bell peppers, wrapped in bacon and basted with barbeque sauce. It was rather over-the-top—it was, after all, inspired by the excesses of early Epic Meal Time videos on YouTube and the BBQ Pit Boys. Of course, it debuted on my show long before I was keto, but I realized it was perfect for the diet once you took away the sugary BBQ sauce. This recipe is perfect for those who don't want a long meal prep and is a great way to get in your protein and fat macros for the day. Plus, who can turn down this much bacon?

500 grams ground pork

Salt, to taste

½ tablespoon black pepper

1 tablespoon paprika

½ tablespoon cayenne pepper

2 tablespoons Italian seasoning

25 grams cheddar cheese, grated

10 grams spring onion, chopped

20 grams mixed bell peppers, diced

6 strips bacon

3 tablespoons Barbeque Sauce
(see page 21)

1   Season the pork with salt, pepper, paprika, cayenne pepper, and Italian seasoning.

2   Cover a cutting board with plastic wrap and spread the pork mixture to form a square. In the center of the square, lay down the cheese, spring onion, and bell peppers.

3   Using the plastic wrap, roll the meat into the shape of a fat log and set carefully into the fridge, being sure to pack it tightly. Allow to chill for 30 minutes.

4   Preheat the oven to 390°F.

5   Organize the strips of bacon on the cutting board until they form a square to wrap around the pork. Take the meat out of the fridge, take off the plastic wrap, and set on top of the bacon. Then, carefully fold and wrap the bacon around the roll.

6   Brush and cover the log with the sauce. Place on a wire rack in a baking sheet, place in the oven, and bake for 45 minutes, removing the meatloaf to baste with more of the sauce after 20 minutes.

7   Remove from the oven and allow to rest for 15 to 20 minutes before cutting and serving.

NUTRITION INFO:
(per serving)

CALORIES: 61
NET CARBS: 5 g
CARBS: 6 g

FAT: 39 g
PROTEIN: 49 g
FIBER: 1 g

BEEF BOURGUIGNON

This dish uses Burgundy wine, but feel free to substitute that with a good red of your choice—good being the operative word here, as the French adage to not cook with any wine you wouldn't drink holds true in this recipe. This is one of those comfort foods that is perfect for a cold winter evening, paired with a glass of red and a book of poetry. I kid—you'd probably get stew all over the book because you'll be too busy scarfing it down.

200 grams smoked bacon cubes

1 kg chuck roast or another cut of beef meant for braising, cut into bite-sized pieces

Salt and pepper, to taste

150 grams onions, chopped

15 grams of butter

400 grams white mushrooms, chopped

¼ teaspoon cayenne pepper

10 grams garlic, minced

236 ml red wine

1 beef bouillon cube or 300 ml beef stock

1 bouquet garni

300 ml water

¼ teaspoon xanthan gum (optional)

1 tablespoon fresh chives, chopped, for garnish

Sour cream, for garnish

1. Place the bacon in a cold Dutch oven or a deep, heavy-bottomed saucepan. Once fully cooked, remove from the pan with a slotted spoon.

2. Season the beef with salt and pepper, then sear in batches in the residual bacon fat until browned all over. Set aside.

3. In the same pan, add in the onions and butter and fry until the onions start to soften. For a richer flavor you can cook the onions until they start to brown.

4. Add in the mushrooms, lightly season with salt and the cayenne pepper, add in the garlic, and cook until the mushrooms release their liquid and start to dry up.

5. Next, add the red wine, bouillon or stock, and bouquet garni and stir. Then, add in the beef and the resting juices from the bacon.

6. Add water until the beef is completely submerged and bring it up to a boil. Once boiling, cover with the lid, reduce the heat to low, and cook for 90 minutes, or place in the oven and cook for 3 hours at 355°F, stirring every 30 minutes. For a thicker stew, add the xanthan gum before covering the pan.

7. Once the meat is fork tender, remove the bouquet garni, and garnish with chives. Serve with a dollop of sour cream on the top.

TIP: To make a bouquet garni, cut a square of cheesecloth, press together parsley, thyme, rosemary and bay leaves in it, then tie up the ends of the cloth to make a little parcel.

SERVINGS: 5
PREP TIME: 10 Minutes
COOKING TIME: 40 Minutes

NUTRITION INFO:
(per serving)

CALORIES: 590
NET CARBS: 6 g
CARBS: 7 g

FAT: 43 g
PROTEIN: 50 g
FIBER: 1 g

BEEF STROGANOFF

Back in the '80s and early '90s, fancy restaurants in India had two sections on the menu: Indian and "continental." Continental included everything from coq au vin and lasagna to lobster thermidor and crêpes Suzette—basically the best-known dishes from around the world, never mind that they tasted nothing like the real thing. Beef stroganoff was one dish I adored from this menu, as we didn't eat much beef at home, especially not in a creamy, delicious sauce. While eating a stroganoff in Russia is still on my bucket list, hopefully this comes close to the real thing.

800 grams chuck roast or any cut of beef meant for braising, cut into long strips

Salt and pepper, to taste

1 tablespoon olive oil

15 grams butter

100 grams onions, sliced

200 grams white mushrooms, sliced

1 teaspoon paprika

½ teaspoon cayenne pepper

500 ml water

75 grams sour cream

50 grams heavy cream

Fresh chives, chopped, for garnish

1   Season the beef with salt and pepper. Heat the olive oil in a Dutch oven and, working in batches, sear the beef until it is browned all over.

2   Remove the beef from the pan and set aside. Add the butter, onions, and mushrooms and sauté. Season with salt, pepper, paprika, and cayenne pepper.

3   Add water and return the beef to the pan. Cover and cook until the beef is fork tender and the liquid has reduced by half or more.

4   Add in the sour cream and heavy cream and mix until well combined. Garnish with chives and serve.

SERVINGS: 4
PREP TIME: 10 Minutes
COOKING TIME: 40 Minutes

NUTRITION INFO:
(per serving)

CALORIES: 503
NET CARBS: 7 g
CARBS: 11 g

FAT: 32 g
PROTEIN: 39 g
FIBER: 4 g

CHILI CON CARNE

Despite my Indian heritage, I don't like spicy food and my tolerance for it is rather low, which explains why I was never the biggest fan of Mexican or Tex-Mex food either—begone damned jalapeños! My wife, though, loves the stuff and she was the one who introduced me to how amazing Tex-Mex food can be. This Texan staple has been one of my absolute favorite meals ever since. This version includes bacon and spinach as a way to include fat and greens, but feel free to leave it out.

200 grams bacon, chopped or cubed

1 tablespoon olive oil

100 grams onions, chopped

2 to 3 garlic cloves, minced

75 grams green bell peppers, chopped

500 grams ground beef

Salt, to taste

1 teaspoon pepper

1 teaspoon cayenne pepper

1 teaspoon cumin powder

1 teaspoon paprika

200 grams tomatoes, pureed

200 grams white mushrooms, sliced

100 grams spinach

1 beef bouillon cube

500 ml water

Fresh oregano, to taste

Fresh cilantro, chopped, to taste

Sour cream, for serving

Avocado, chopped, for serving

1 Fry the bacon in the olive oil, starting with a cold pan so that the fat renders out. Then, add in the onions and fry.

2 Once the onions are translucent, add the garlic and brown. Then, add the green peppers.

3 Add in the beef along with all the dry seasonings and cook until the meat starts to brown.

4 Add in the tomatoes, mushrooms, and spinach, mix, and cook for 2 minutes until the spinach starts to wilt. Add the bouillon cube and water and cook down for 10 minutes.

5 Add in the fresh oregano and cilantro and cook until the sauce reduces, if desired.

6 Serve with sour cream and fresh avocado.

SERVINGS: 5
PREP TIME: 10 Minutes
COOKING TIME: 35 Minutes

NUTRITION INFO:
(per serving)

CALORIES: 311
NET CARBS: 7 g
CARBS: 10 g

FAT: 16 g
PROTEIN: 30 g
FIBER: 3 g

COTTAGE PIE

Shepherd's pie—minced meat topped with mashed potato—is made with ground lamb. When it's made with ground beef, it becomes a cottage pie. This one gets the keto makeover with—you guessed it—our old friend, the cauliflower. Is it just as delicious? Of course!

500 grams cauliflower, chopped

2 egg yolks

50 grams Parmesan cheese, plus more for topping

Salt and pepper, to taste

2 tablespoons butter

1 tablespoon olive oil

50 grams onions, chopped

10 grams garlic, minced

500 grams ground beef

1 beef stock cube

1 teaspoon Worcestershire sauce

50 ml tomato puree

½ tablespoon fresh rosemary, minced

½ tablespoon dried thyme

100 grams white mushrooms, diced

100 grams spinach

150 ml water

1 Microwave, steam, or boil the cauliflower until tender, then transfer to a food processor and blend until smooth. Add the egg yolks and cheese, season with salt and pepper, and blend until smooth. Set aside.

2 Melt the butter and olive oil in a pan, then add the onions and fry until golden brown. Add the garlic and cook until just beginning to brown, then add in the beef and continue cooking.

3 Preheat the oven to 390°F. Once the beef starts to brown, add in the beef stock cube, Worcestershire sauce, tomato puree, rosemary, and thyme. Mix and cook for 2 to 3 minutes.

4 Add in the mushrooms and spinach, season to taste, and cook until the spinach is wilted. Once wilted, add water and cook for 10 minutes.

5 Add the meat mixture to a casserole dish, layer the cauliflower puree on top, sprinkle with additional Parmesan, and bake for 15 minutes. Serve warm.

SERVINGS (SQUID AND SAUCE): 2

SERVINGS (MEATBALLS): 10
(1 serving = 1 meatball)

PREP TIME: 15 Minutes

COOKING TIME: 30 Minutes

NUTRITION INFO:
(per serving of squid and sauce)

CALORIES: 206   **FAT:** 14 g

NET CARBS: 6 g   **PROTEIN:** 13 g

CARBS: 7 g   **FIBER:** 1 g

NUTRITION INFO:
(per meatball)

CALORIES: 139   **FAT:** 10g

NET CARBS: 0 g   **PROTEIN:** 11 g

CARBS: 0 g   **FIBER:** 0 g

SPAGHETTI AND MEATBALLS

At some point on my keto journey, I got tired of spiralized zucchini in lieu of pasta and I started looking for other options. One of my friends threw me a challenge: make a no-carb spaghetti, and not with shirataki noodles. He suggested I use squid to make noodles (or "squoodles," as I call them), and this recipe was born.

1 For the meatballs, mix together the beef, pork, cheeses, seasonings, and the egg. Using an ice cream scoop or a scale, portion out the meatballs and shape. Add the oil to a pan and fry until browned all over and cooked through. Set aside.

2 To make the spaghetti and sauce, add the butter and olive oil to the pan, being sure not to wipe out the pan after cooking the meatballs. Fry the mushrooms, then season with salt, pepper, chili flakes, and oregano.

3 Add in the tomatoes and water, cover, and cook for 5 to 7 minutes. Once the tomato sauce has reduced, add additional salt, if desired.

4 Add the squid and cook for 2 minutes. Be careful not to overcook. Finish with fresh basil and serve the squid and tomato sauce with the meatballs.

For the Meatballs

250 grams ground beef

250 grams ground pork

30 grams Parmesan cheese, grated

15 grams cheddar cheese, grated

1 tablespoon fresh parsley, minced

1 teaspoon fresh thyme, minced

1 teaspoon garlic powder

½ teaspoon cayenne pepper

½ teaspoon black pepper powder

1 teaspoon salt

1 egg

1 tablespoon olive oil, for frying

For the Spaghetti and Tomato Sauce

1 tablespoon butter

1 tablespoon olive oil

60 grams white mushrooms, chopped

1 teaspoon salt

½ teaspoon pepper

½ teaspoon red chili flakes

1 teaspoon dried oregano

100 grams tomatoes

50 ml water

150 grams squid, tubes cut into long strips

1 tablespoon fresh basil, minced

SERVINGS: 2
PREP TIME: 10 Minutes
COOKING TIME: 10 Minutes

NUTRITION INFO:
(per serving)

CALORIES: 409
NET CARBS: 2 g
CARBS: 5 g

FAT: 25 g
PROTEIN: 39 g
FIBER: 3 g

WIENER SCHNITZEL

For the longest time, I thought the "wiener" in "wiener schnitzel" stood for sausage, so you can imagine my confusion when I ordered it abroad and got a cutlet instead. Later I found out that "wiener" means "Viennese" and "schnitzel" referred to a flattened, tenderized meat cutlet. It was quite the aha moment. My version uses keto-friendly Bread Crumbs (see page 25) and some Master Chef inspiration for the flavoring.

100 grams Bread Crumbs (see page 25)

1 tablespoon fresh parsley, chopped

1 teaspoon garlic powder

30 grams Parmesan cheese, grated

260 grams veal cutlets

Salt and pepper, to taste

1 egg

Olive oil or lard, for frying

Fresh greens, for serving

1 lemon slice, for garnish

1   Mix the Bread Crumbs, chopped parsley, garlic powder, and Parmesan cheese.

2   Spread the veal on a chopping board or counter and lay a sheet of plastic wrap on top. Using a meat tenderizer, pound the cutlets until it is as thin as possible. Then, season with salt and pepper on both sides.

3   Beat the egg in a bowl, then dip the veal cutlets first into the egg, and then into the Bread Crumbs until coated.

4   Heat the olive oil or lard in a skillet. Deep fry the cutlets over medium heat until they're golden brown and cooked through. Serve with fresh greens and garnish with a slice of lemon.

SERVINGS: 5
PREP TIME: 5 Minutes
COOKING TIME: 35 Minutes

NUTRITION INFO:
(per serving)

CALORIES: 569
NET CARBS: 1 g
CARBS: 1 g

FAT: 47 g
PROTEIN: 30 g
FIBER: 0 g

BARBEQUE PORK SPARERIBS

Another of my grandfather's signature recipes, these ribs are much loved in my family. We always used the pressure cooker in India to cook tough cuts of meat. A lot of that has to do with the fact that people live in apartments and there's no room to barbeque or grill meats. So while some people might scoff at the idea of pressure-cooked ribs, once you see that meat fall off the bone and you taste that tangy BBQ sauce, you'll be giving this dish the thumbs, or rather, horns up!

1 kg pork spareribs

Salt, to taste

1 cinnamon stick

1 bay leaf

8 peppercorns

2 star anise

10 grams garlic, minced

10 grams ginger, minced

1 tablespoon five-spice powder

4 tablespoons Barbeque Sauce
(see page 21)

1   Pressure cook the ribs with salt, a cinnamon stick, bay leaf, peppercorns, star anise, garlic, and ginger for 30 minutes until tender.

2   Remove the ribs from the cooker and strain out the juices from the pressure cooker. This can be saved for use in future recipes.

3   Next, mix the cooked ribs in a bowl with the five-spice powder and sauce. Add salt as needed, then pan fry the ribs for 2 to 3 minutes per side until a crust forms. Serve.

NUTRITION INFO:

(per serving)

CALORIES: 206
NET CARBS: 6 g
CARBS: 10 g

FAT: 16 g
PROTEIN: 6 g
FIBER: 4 g

CHORIZO PILAF

Chorizo is another one of those beautiful foods that my wife introduced me to. I wouldn't eat the local Goan sausage, which is a fiery version of the Portuguese chouriço, so she'd make a badass chorizo pulao or pilaf (not keto, of course) with Spanish or Iberico chorizo. Even though rice was no longer in my diet I didn't want to miss out on that great pulao. So I turned to my good pal cauliflower to fill the void, and it definitely did the job.

50 grams Spanish chorizo or Portuguese chouriço, cubed

1 tablespoon olive oil

½ teaspoon cumin seeds

30 grams onion, chopped

1 teaspoon ginger-garlic paste

50 grams tomato, chopped

½ teaspoon turmeric

½ teaspoon Kashmiri red chili powder (or sweet paprika)

Salt, to taste

250 grams cooked cauliflower rice

Fresh cilantro, chopped, for garnish

1   Fry the chorizo in the olive oil until it starts to crisp and release its oils. Then, add in the cumin seeds, onion, and ginger-garlic paste and cook until the onion is soft.

2   Add in the tomato, turmeric, chili powder or paprika, and a splash of water and cook for 3 to 4 minutes. Add salt to taste, then add another splash of water to make a gravy-like consistency.

3   Add the cauliflower rice and mix well until it is completely coated with the juices in the pan. Cook for a minute or two until there is no liquid left in the pan. Garnish with the cilantro and serve.

TIP: To make cauliflower rice, cut 1 large head of cauliflower into chunks and either grate with a box grater or blitz in a food processor. Sauté in 1 tablespoon olive oil until tender.

SERVINGS: 8	NUTRITION INFO:	CALORIES: 548	FAT: 40 g
PREP TIME: 45 Minutes	(per serving)	NET CARBS: 1 g	PROTEIN: 44 g
COOKING TIME: 4 Hours		CARBS: 1 g	FIBER: 0 g

PORK CARNITAS

I have to credit one of my favorite YouTube chefs for inspiring this keto version of carnitas. Chef John from Food Wishes is a personal hero of mine, and the way he uses humor and goodwill to make food and cooking accessible has influenced much of my cooking journey as well. Chef John, this one's for you!

1.5 kg boneless pork shoulder, cut into even chunks

1 teaspoon salt

1 teaspoon black pepper

1 teaspoon ground cumin

½ teaspoon five-spice powder

½ teaspoon cayenne pepper

2 cinnamon sticks

2 bay leaves

5 garlic cloves, minced

Zest and juice of 1 lemon

1. Preheat the oven to 285°F. Rub down and marinate the pork with all the ingredients, for at least 30 minutes, then place in a roasting tray. Cover with foil and cook for 3½ hours.

2. Once the pork is done cooking, remove the tray from the oven, and use a slotted spoon to remove the pork pieces. Set aside.

3. Pour the liquids from the roasting tray into a jar and set aside. The liquid will separate into two layers—the top is fat and the bottom is jus.

4. Put the pork back in the roasting tray and pour some of the fat over it. Return the tray to the oven, uncovered, and turn the broiler on high. Cook for 15 minutes until the outside is crispy.

5. Remove from the oven and serve immediately.

NUTRITION INFO:
(per serving)

CALORIES: 423
NET CARBS: 1 g
CARBS: 2 g

FAT: 30 g
PROTEIN: 33 g
FIBER: 1 g

PORK CHOPS
IN A CREAMY MUSTARD SAUCE

My grandfather was a legend. He was a dexterous hunter who'd go out and shoot game on the weekends. He didn't hunt for sport—he believed in using every part of the animal and taught me to respect where my food came from. He was also an incredible cook. His pork chops were one of his most memorable dishes, thanks to their melt-in-your-mouth texture. It took a long time to get mine perfect like his, but thankfully I inherited his perseverance.

500 grams pork chops

Salt and pepper, to taste

½ teaspoon cayenne pepper

1 tablespoon coconut oil

1 tablespoon garlic-and-herb butter

1 green bell pepper, chopped

117 ml water

1 tablespoon mustard

100 ml heavy cream

35 grams cheddar cheese, grated

1 spring onion green, chopped,
for garnish

1 Score the layer of fat on the outside of each chop. Season generously with salt, pepper, and cayenne pepper.

2 Heat the coconut oil in a pan and, once nearly smoking, add in the pork chops and cook for 2 minutes per side, or slightly longer for thicker chops.

3 Turn chops so they are fat-side down and cook for an additional 2 minutes until the fat has partially rendered.

4 Lay the chops back down and add the garlic-and-herb butter (or use regular butter and add minced garlic and herbs to taste). Baste the chops with the melted butter until they are firm to the touch with a slight amount of spring. Remove from the pan and set aside.

5 Drain excess fat from pan, then sauté the bell pepper in the remainder. Once the peppers have softened, deglaze the pan with water and add the mustard and the resting juice from the chops. Stir together.

6 Add the cream and cheese to the mixture and stir until the cheese melts.

7 Cover the pork chops with the sauce, garnish with spring onion greens, and serve.

SERVINGS: 4
PREP TIME: 10 Minutes
COOKING TIME: 20 Minutes

NUTRITION INFO:
(per serving)

CALORIES: 274
NET CARBS: 6 g
CARBS: 11 g

FAT: 18 g
PROTEIN: 20 g
FIBER: 5 g

PORK FRIED RICE

I'm often asked what my favorite keto meal is, and this dish has always been my answer. It's everything I could ask for in a single dish: Asian inspiration meets Italian cooking, low-carb cauliflower rice, assorted veggies, porky goodness, and tons and tons of flavor. What more is there to want?

1 tablespoon olive oil

1 tablespoon butter

1 spring onion, whites and greens separated, chopped

250 grams ground pork

2 garlic cloves, chopped

1 teaspoon salt

½ teaspoon pepper

½ teaspoon paprika

¼ teaspoon cayenne pepper

1 teaspoon dried oregano

½ teaspoon red chili flakes

100 grams mixed bell peppers, chopped

200 grams baby spinach

500 grams cooked cauliflower rice (see page 149)

50 grams cheddar cheese, grated

30 ml heavy cream

Fresh parsley, chopped, to taste, plus more for garnish

8 to 10 olives, chopped

Parmesan cheese, grated, for garnish

1   Heat the olive oil and butter in a large frying pan. Add in the spring onion whites and the ground pork and fry, making sure to stir and break the pork to avoid lumping.

2   Add the garlic, season the pork with salt, pepper, paprika, cayenne pepper, oregano, and chili flakes, and add in the bell peppers and spinach. Sauté until the spinach wilts.

3   Add in the cauliflower rice and mix. Add in the cheese, heavy cream, parsley, and spring onion greens and mix again.

4   Mix in the chopped olives, garnish with Parmesan and additional parsley, and serve.

NUTRITION INFO:
(per serving)

CALORIES: 471
NET CARBS: 1 g
CARBS: 1 g

FAT: 34 g
PROTEIN: 39 g
FIBER: 0 g

PULLED PORK

I haven't been to America yet, but I've long been fascinated by the American food scene thanks to TV shows and YouTube videos. Texas BBQ can always seize my attention. I can't begin to count how long I've spent drooling over hunks of meat roasted over a smoky BBQ. This recipe is an homage to that American tradition.

1 kg bone-in pork shoulder

1 tablespoon olive oil

2 teaspoons salt

1 teaspoon pepper

1 teaspoon paprika

1 teaspoon cayenne pepper

1 teaspoon garlic powder

½ teaspoon five-spice powder

½ teaspoon cinnamon powder

½ teaspoon stevia or keto-friendly sweetener of choice

1 Preheat the oven to 300°F. Rub the pork with oil. Then, mix the seasonings together and rub them into the pork.

2 Put the pork on a wire rack in a baking sheet. Fill the sheet with about 1 inch of water, cover with foil, and cook for 2 hours.

3 Once done, remove the foil and put the pork back in the oven for 10 minutes at 390°F to crisp up the fat.

4 Remove the pork from the bone, shred, and serve.

TIP: You could use this in myriad ways—toss it through some Barbeque Sauce (see page 21) and eat it as it is, make sandwiches with it using keto bread, throw it into cauliflower rice (see page 149) and make pulled pork fried rice, fill a keto wrap with it, or even turn it into a salad!

SERVINGS: 3
PREP TIME: 40 Minutes
COOKING TIME: 25 Minutes

NUTRITION INFO:
(per serving)

CALORIES: 509
NET CARBS: 5 g
CARBS: 6 g

FAT: 34 g
PROTEIN: 40 g
FIBER: 1 g

CHICKEN
IN MUSHROOM AND WINE SAUCE

Not all recipes need to be complex and take ages to cook to be delicious. I love the simplicity of this dish, and how you can pack so much flavor into the sauce. It's simple, elegant, and perfect for making in big batches to provide you with a week's worth of meals.

500 grams boneless chicken leg and thigh meat

2 tablespoons olive oil

Salt and pepper, to taste

1 teaspoon fresh rosemary, minced

1 teaspoon fresh thyme, minced

1 tablespoon butter

200 grams mushrooms

100 ml white wine

10 grams garlic, minced

1 chicken bouillon cube or 100 ml chicken stock

100 ml water

100 ml heavy cream

1 teaspoon fresh parsley, minced, plus more for garnish

50 grams cheddar cheese, grated

1 Marinate the chicken with 1 tablespoon olive oil, salt, pepper, rosemary, and thyme for at least 30 minutes. Heat the remaining olive oil in a frying pan and fry the chicken on both sides until it starts to brown.

2 Add butter to the pan and baste the chicken with the melted butter while cooking. Then, remove the chicken, add the chopped mushrooms to the pan, and fry.

3 Deglaze the pan with the white wine and cook down, then add in the garlic and bouillon cube (or stock) and cook down further. Once the mushrooms and garlic have browned a bit, add in the resting juices from the chicken and water to deglaze the pan.

4 Add in the cream and parsley and mix well. Return the chicken to the pan to soak in the sauce to finish cooking. Top with the cheese and additional parsley.

SERVINGS: 4
PREP TIME: 10 Minutes
COOKING TIME: 15 Minutes

NUTRITION INFO:
(per serving)

CALORIES: 491
NET CARBS: 4 g
CARBS: 5 g

FAT: 28 g
PROTEIN: 41 g
FIBER: 1 g

CHICKEN
IN MUSHROOM SAUCE

If it isn't already evident, if I had to pair chicken with one veggie it would be mushrooms. Mushrooms and creamy sauces are a match made in keto heaven, and this savory dish is ideal for when you need a quick, comforting dinner.

2 skinless, boneless chicken breasts, butterflied

Salt and pepper, to taste

¼ teaspoon paprika

1 tablespoon olive oil

1 tablespoon butter

100 grams white mushrooms, chopped

Fresh thyme, minced, to taste

2 garlic cloves, minced

50 ml water

60 grams Swiss cheese, grated

100 ml heavy cream

Fresh parsley, chopped, to taste

1 Season the chicken breasts with salt, pepper, and paprika on both sides.

2 Heat the olive oil in a pan and fry the chicken for 2 minutes on each side over high heat, then remove from the pan.

3 In the same pan, add the butter and mushrooms and season with salt. Add in the thyme and garlic and cook until the mushrooms release their liquid.

4 Add the water and cheese and stir until melted. Add in the cream, mix well, and cook until the sauce reaches the desired consistency. Finish the sauce with fresh parsley.

5 Slice the chicken breasts, pour the sauce on top, and serve.

SERVINGS: 2
PREP TIME: 10 Minutes
COOKING TIME: 25 Minutes

NUTRITION INFO:
(per serving)

CALORIES: 477
NET CARBS: 3 g
CARBS: 4 g

FAT: 32 g
PROTEIN: 47 g
FIBER: 1 g

CHICKEN PARMESAN

When I went to Italy, I was mystified that I couldn't find chicken parmigiana on any menu. Of course, I now know it is actually an Italian-American dish that is a cross between a breaded cutlet and Italian melanzane alla parmigiana (eggplant Parmesan). I didn't want to do yet another breaded dish, so I skipped the breadcrumbs and instead coated the chicken with fresh parsley and Parmesan cheese. The result is definitely winner, winner, chicken dinner.

300 grams skinless, boneless chicken breasts, butterflied

Salt and pepper, to taste

½ egg

1 teaspoon Italian seasoning

30 grams Parmesan cheese, grated

1 tablespoon fresh parsley, minced

1 tablespoon olive oil

1 tablespoon butter

5 grams garlic, minced

100 grams tomatoes, pureed

1 teaspoon dried oregano

½ teaspoon red chili flakes

1 tablespoon fresh basil, minced

100 grams mozzarella cheese, grated

1. Cover the chicken breasts with plastic wrap and beat with a meat tenderizer until evenly thin. Season with salt and pepper on both sides.

2. Beat the egg with the Italian seasoning to make an egg wash. Then, mix together the grated Parmesan cheese and chopped parsley to create the bread crumbs.

3. Dip the chicken into the egg wash, then coat with the Parmesan mixture. Pan fry the chicken breasts with the olive oil and half the butter. Cook for 60 to 90 seconds on each side. Set aside.

4. Add the garlic to the same pan and cook until lightly browned. Next, add in the tomatoes, salt, oregano, and chili flakes.

5. Add the remaining butter, cover, and cook over medium heat for 4 to 5 minutes. Finish the sauce with the basil.

6. To assemble the chicken Parmesan, layer an ovenproof dish with the tomato sauce, place the chicken on top, and top with mozzarella.

7. Broil in the oven for 7 to 8 minutes at the highest temperature to melt and brown the cheese, then serve.

SERVINGS: 2
PREP TIME: 5 Minutes
COOKING TIME: 30 Minutes

NUTRITION INFO:
(per serving)

CALORIES: 546
NET CARBS: 5 g
CARBS: 6 g

FAT: 41 g
PROTEIN: 39 g
FIBER: 1 g

CHICKEN THIGHS WITH MUSTARD GRAVY

Chicken skin is delicious and full of good fat, but you won't find a single Indian dish with it. You have to specifically ask for chicken with skin at most butcher shops. This is unfortunate, since chicken skin crisps incredibly well and is nearly irresistible when paired with mustard gravy.

4 skin-on, bone-in chicken thighs,
½ teaspoon salt
½ teaspoon pepper
½ teaspoon smoked paprika
1 tablespoon olive oil
1 tablespoon butter
30 grams red onion, chopped
10 grams garlic, chopped
1 tablespoon white wine vinegar
100 ml chicken stock
1 teaspoon whole grain mustard
1 teaspoon Dijon mustard
50 ml heavy cream
1 tablespoon fresh parsley, minced

1   Season the chicken thighs with salt, pepper, and paprika on both sides.

2   Heat a stainless-steel pan and add in the olive oil when hot. Then, place the chicken thighs skin-side down in the pan and cook over high or medium-high heat for 4 to 5 minutes, or until the skin is crispy. Cook for an additional 2 minutes, remove from the pan, and set aside.

3   In the same pan, add the butter and, once it has frothed, add in the red onion and garlic and cook until translucent and soft.

4   Deglaze the pan with the white wine vinegar and the chicken stock. Add in the mustards and stir until a sauce begins to form.

5   Place the chicken pieces skin-side up in the pan, cover, and cook for about 8 minutes. Remove the thighs, stir in the cream and parsley to finish the sauce, and spoon it over the thighs.

SERVINGS: 4
PREP TIME: 10 Minutes
COOKING TIME: 35 Minutes

NUTRITION INFO:
(per serving)

CALORIES: 785
NET CARBS: 4 g
CARBS: 5 g

FAT: 64 g
PROTEIN: 61 g
FIBER: 1 g

COQ AU VIN

While I'm not a big wine drinker, I'm more than happy to cook with it. Wine adds so much complexity to food, and I absolutely love the rich sauce it creates in this classic French dish. The "coq" in this dish's name comes from the tradition of cooking roosters—these tough, old birds benefitted from the long braising and cooking time—but today almost everyone uses good ol' chicken.

200 grams smoked bacon cubes or lardons

4 full skin-on chicken legs

Salt and pepper, to taste

200 grams white mushrooms, sliced

100 grams pearl onions

A bunch of fresh thyme sprigs

150 ml dry red wine

200 ml chicken stock

⅛ teaspoon xanthan gum (optional)

Fresh parsley, chopped, for garnish

1   Fry the bacon in a skillet or frying pan until nice and crispy, then set aside.

2   Season the chicken legs with salt and pepper and fry in the residual bacon fat, basting the chicken until crispy. Once they are a nice golden brown, remove and set aside.

3   In the same pan, sauté the mushrooms and onions and season with salt and pepper.

4   Once the vegetables start to brown, add in the thyme and deglaze with wine.

5   Return the chicken to the pan, add the stock and half the bacon, then cover and let cook until the chicken is tender and cooked through.

6   Once cooked, remove the chicken legs and reduce the sauce to the desired consistency. For a thicker sauce, add the xanthan gum.

7   Once the sauce is ready, add the chicken and garnish with the remaining bacon and fresh parsley.

SERVINGS: 5
PREP TIME: 30 Minutes
COOKING TIME: 30 Minutes

NUTRITION INFO:
(per serving)

CALORIES: 290
NET CARBS: 3 g
CARBS: 3 g

FAT: 15 g
PROTEIN: 28 g
FIBER: 0 g

CREAMY CHICKEN CURRY

By now you know that I wasn't always the biggest fan of Indian food. I never went to an Indian restaurant by choice, nor did I cook any Indian food, mainly because I was scared of the spice levels in the recipes. All that changed in 2011 when I had drummer George Kollias on my show. I realized I didn't want to feed him bacon bombs and burgers, so I started to explore the cuisine I had avoided for all those years. That led to this curry recipe, one that I am incredibly proud of.

1 whole chicken, skin removed, cut into breasts, thighs, and drumsticks

2 teaspoons ginger-garlic paste

½ tablespoon fresh lime juice

1 teaspoon salt

1 teaspoon red chili powder

1 teaspoon turmeric

½ teaspoon garam masala

1 teaspoon ground coriander

2 tablespoons butter

50 grams onion, chopped

1 teaspoon cumin

3 whole cloves

3 cardamom pods

10 grams almonds

50 ml tomato puree

200 ml water, plus more as needed

10 grams fresh cilantro, chopped, for garnish

50 ml heavy cream, for garnish

1 Marinate the chicken with half the ginger-garlic paste, lime juice, salt, red chili powder, turmeric, garam masala, and ground coriander for 20 to 30 minutes.

2 Melt half of the butter in a pan and add the onion, cumin, cloves, and cardamom. Cook until the onion turns translucent, then add the rest of the ginger-garlic paste and almonds and cook for another 2 minutes.

3 Add in the tomato puree and cook for 5 minutes, adding water as needed to prevent burning. Then, transfer the mixture to a blender and puree.

4 In the same pan add the remaining butter and fry the chicken. After about 5 minutes of cooking, deglaze with water and add the blended curry paste. Thin the curry with additional water to reach the desired consistency.

5 Cover and cook for 10 minutes or until chicken is cooked through. Garnish with the cilantro and cream and serve.

SERVINGS: 1
PREP TIME: 10 Minutes
COOKING TIME: 10 Minutes

NUTRITION INFO:
(per serving)

CALORIES: 563
NET CARBS: 2 g
CARBS: 2 g

FAT: 38 g
PROTEIN: 39 g
FIBER: 0 g

CREAMY PESTO CHICKEN

Basil Pesto is a quick way to add an explosion of flavor to almost any meat. Even though this recipe is similar to my Pesto Grilled Chicken with Mushrooms (see page 177), the addition of the cheesy, creamy goodness creates a completely different dish that'll knock your socks off. This makes a great one-person meal as is, or can be scaled up for a family dinner. Just be sure to make enough for seconds.

1 skinless, boneless chicken breast

Salt and pepper, to taste

1 tablespoon olive oil

50 ml water

1 tablespoon Basil Pesto (see page 22)

30 grams Parmesan cheese, grated

50 ml heavy cream

1 Beat the chicken with the flat side of a meat tenderizer until flat, then season with salt and pepper on both sides.

2 Heat the olive oil in a pan and fry the chicken for 2 minutes on each side over high heat. Then, deglaze the pan with water.

3 Add in the pesto and mix well, adding more pepper to taste. Add in the cheese and cream and cook until well mixed. Pour in the resting juices from the chicken and stir.

4 Slice the chicken, pour the sauce on top, and serve.

SERVINGS: 4
PREP TIME: 10 Minutes
COOKING TIME: 10 Minutes

NUTRITION INFO:
(per serving)

CALORIES: 358
NET CARBS: 1 g
CARBS: 2 g

FAT: 20 g
PROTEIN: 43 g
FIBER: 1 g

FRIED CHICKEN

Everybody's favorite hangover snack, Sunday dinner, and mid-week indulgence, fried chicken comes with as much guilt as grease. For so long we've been told that it's clogging our arteries and making us obese. But what if we take away the things that make it unhealthy, give it a keto-friendly breading, and turn it into a meal that hits all the macros? That's exactly what this recipe does while still retaining that signature crunch we know and love.

1 teaspoon salt

1 teaspoon pepper

1 teaspoon smoked paprika

½ teaspoon cayenne pepper

1 teaspoon garlic powder

4 skinless, boneless chicken breasts

1 egg

100 grams Bread Crumbs (see page 25)

Cooking fat of choice, for deep frying

1 Mix the salt, pepper, paprika, cayenne pepper, and garlic powder in a bowl, then season the chicken breasts on both sides with the mixture.

2 Beat the egg in a bowl, then dip each breast into first the egg, then the Bread Crumbs until coated.

3 Place 2 inches of your chosen cooking fat in a Dutch oven and bring to 350°F. Deep fry the chicken for about 3 to 4 minutes until the outside is golden brown and the chicken is cooked through. Serve immediately.

SERVINGS: 2
PREP TIME: 5 Minutes
COOKING TIME: 15 Minutes

NUTRITION INFO:
(per serving)

CALORIES: 426
NET CARBS: 1 g
CARBS: 1 g

FAT: 24 g
PROTEIN: 52 g
FIBER: 0 g

LEMON PEPPER CHICKEN

According to my wife, this dish convinced her I was a keeper. My relatives would come from America and bring us giant jars of lemon pepper seasoning, and it was the easiest thing to throw together with some chicken, cheese, and cream for a delectable dish. Even when I knew nothing about cooking, I knew this dish was a keeper.

300 grams skinless, boneless chicken breasts

2 teaspoons lemon pepper seasoning

1 tablespoon olive oil

50 to 60 ml water

50 grams cheddar cheese, grated

50 ml heavy cream

Salt, to taste

1 teaspoon fresh chives, diced

1 teaspoon fresh parsley, minced

1 Season the chicken on both sides with the lemon pepper seasoning.

2 Heat the olive oil in a pan and fry the chicken for 3 to 4 minutes on each side, or until golden brown.

3 Deglaze the pan with water, then sprinkle in the cheese and cream. Mix well until the cheese is melted and the mixture forms a sauce. Salt to taste.

4 Finish the sauce with chives and parsley and serve.

SERVINGS: 1	**NUTRITION INFO:**	**CALORIES:** 475	**FAT:** 34 g
PREP TIME: 40 Minutes	(per serving)	**NET CARBS:** 4 g	**PROTEIN:** 38 g
COOKING TIME: 15 Minutes		**CARBS:** 5 g	**FIBER:** 1 g

PESTO GRILLED CHICKEN WITH MUSHROOMS

I like to think the hallmark of my cooking is simple and delicious food, and I consider this dish to be a prime example. The Basil Pesto infuses the chicken and mushrooms with incredible flavor for a meal that's perfect for those days you'd rather not spend hours cooking.

1 skinless, boneless chicken breast

100 grams whole white mushrooms

1 tablespoon Basil Pesto (see page 22)

Salt, to taste

1 tablespoon olive oil

1 tablespoon water

½ teaspoon red chili flakes

1 Marinate the chicken and whole mushrooms in the pesto, for at least 30 minutes, and season with salt.

2 Heat the olive oil in a pan, add in the chicken and mushrooms, and fry the chicken for about 3 to 4 minutes per side or until cooked through. Remember to stir the mushrooms while cooking the chicken to avoid burning. Remove the chicken from the pan and set aside.

3 Add the water to deglaze the pan and stir the mushrooms. Pour in the resting juices from the chicken and cook down until you have a jus-like consistency. Turn off the heat.

4 Sprinkle the chili flakes over the chicken and mushrooms and serve.

TIP: If you have the time, leave the chicken and mushrooms to marinate for an hour to really enhance the flavor.

SERVINGS: 2
PREP TIME: 5 Minutes
COOKING TIME: 15 Minutes

NUTRITION INFO:
(per serving)

CALORIES: 392
NET CARBS: 7 g
CARBS: 9 g

FAT: 32 g
PROTEIN: 18 g
FIBER: 2 g

FISH
IN LEMON AND CAPER BUTTER SAUCE

It took a real shift in mind-set to get comfortable being generous with butter. That's exactly what this recipe celebrates—that move from "fat is bad" to enjoying the innate goodness of all things butter. The fresh acidity of the lemon really cuts through the richness of the butter in this easy-to-make meal.

15 ml olive oil

250 grams salmon fillets or fish of choice

Salt and pepper, to taste

50 grams small red onions, chopped

80 grams butter

10 grams garlic cloves, minced

15 grams capers

5 grams fresh parsley, minced

Fresh lemon juice, to taste

1 Heat the olive oil in a pan. Then, season the fish with salt and pepper and fry until fully cooked. Set aside.

2 Add onions to the pan and cook until translucent, then turn the heat to low and add in half the butter. Cook until the butter has finished frothing, then add the garlic and capers, being sure to break the capers with a spatula.

3 Turn off the heat and add in the remaining butter, parsley, and lemon juice.

4 Mix well and, once the butter has melted, pour over the fish and serve.

NUTRITION INFO:
(per serving)

CALORIES: 470

NET CARBS: 8 g

CARBS: 13 g

FAT: 36 g

PROTEIN: 31 g

FIBER: 5 g

PRAWN
RISOTTO

I've always heard that mixing dairy and seafood is a no-no, but this recipe proves that convention wrong. Cauliflower rice meets a creamy sauce and beautifully cooked prawns in a delicious faux risotto that would give the real thing a run for its money.

100 grams oyster or porcini mushrooms, chopped

2 tablespoons olive oil

1 tablespoon butter

300 grams cauliflower rice (see page 149)

Salt and pepper, to taste

150 ml fish stock

1 teaspoon fresh or dried oregano

½ teaspoon red chili flakes

250 grams prawns

100 grams mascarpone cheese

1 tablespoon fresh basil, minced

1 Fry the mushrooms in 1 tablespoon of olive oil until browned. Set aside.

2 In the same pan, heat the remaining olive oil and butter.

3 Add in the cauliflower rice, season with salt and pepper, and cook for 4 minutes, stirring constantly. Add in the stock and cook for another 4 minutes.

4 Season with the oregano and chili flakes. Then, add in the prawns and cook for another 2 minutes until the cauliflower is tender and the prawns are cooked through.

5 Turn off the heat and stir in the mascarpone cheese and mushrooms. Finish with fresh basil and serve.

BAKED ZUCCHINI CASSEROLE

This was one of the first low-carb pasta recipes that I was pleasantly surprised by—I couldn't believe it was zucchini! This recipe was made in the days when I didn't have a spiralizer to make proper zucchini noodles, so I had to fall back on my trusty vegetable peeler. It's arguably one of the easiest casserole recipes ever.

100 grams zucchini noodles
60 ml Marinara Sauce (see page 29)
30 grams salami
1 tablespoon olive oil
50 grams mozzarella cheese, grated

1 Preheat your oven to 390°F. In an ovenproof dish, mix the zucchini, sauce, salami, and olive oil.

2 Cover with cheese and bake for 10 minutes or until the cheese is golden brown. Once browned, remove from the oven and serve.

SERVINGS: 4
PREP TIME: 10 Minutes
COOKING TIME: 35 Minutes

NUTRITION INFO:
(per serving)

CALORIES: 481
NET CARBS: 9 g
CARBS: 12 g

FAT: 43 g
PROTEIN: 17 g
FIBER: 3 g

CAULIFLOWER MAC AND CHEESE

I had a fairly nonstandard upbringing, as my family's cooking was more European-influenced than Indian. Pork chops and mac and cheese were on the menu more than rice, dal, and curry. In fact, my mother's mac and cheese was legendary, and my friends would beg to come over and eat it. My mother never baked her mac and cheese in the oven, but this recipe was begging for a crispy crust. Yes, I know it's technically cauliflower and cheese, but by now you know that cauliflower is whatever you want it to be.

1 small onion, chopped

1 teaspoon garlic butter

100 grams ham, chopped

½ teaspoon red chili flakes

500 grams cauliflower, florets cut from stalks

Salt, to taste

50 grams salted butter

½ teaspoon garlic powder

½ teaspoon cayenne pepper

½ teaspoon grated nutmeg

1 teaspoon fresh thyme, minced

½ chicken bouillon cube

300 ml heavy cream

150 grams cheddar cheese, grated

Pepper, to taste

25 grams pine nuts, crushed

1   Preheat the oven to 390°F. Sweat the onion in a pan with the garlic butter. Once translucent, add the chopped ham and chili flakes and sauté for a few minutes. Set aside.

2   Season the cauliflower florets with salt and microwave for 5 minutes.

3   Melt the salted butter in a saucepan and add in the garlic powder, cayenne, pepper, nutmeg, thyme, and bouillon cube. Mix well.

4   Once the butter has finished frothing, add the cream and mix vigorously. Let it reduce down by about ¼.

5   Add in 100 grams of the cheese and cook until fully melted, then season with pepper.

6   Mix together the cauliflower, ham and onion, and cheese sauce in a bowl. Put the mixture in a casserole dish and top with pine nuts and the remaining cheese.

7   Bake for 10 to 12 minutes in the oven, then broil for 2 minutes to form the crust. Remove from the oven and serve.

SERVINGS: 4
PREP TIME: 40 Minutes
COOKING TIME: 35 Minutes

NUTRITION INFO:
(per serving)

CALORIES: 260
NET CARBS: 5 g
CARBS: 9 g

FAT: 19 g
PROTEIN: 14 g
FIBER: 4 g

EGGPLANT INVOLTINI

I'm so glad, that as an adult, I've discovered a love of vegetables I used to positively hate as a kid, otherwise I would have missed out on dishes like this. These little rolls of eggplant are stuffed with ricotta, doused in marinara, and baked with cheese on top for a sweet and savory dinner. If you can't find ricotta, you can always sub in cottage cheese, though the creaminess of the ricotta really makes this dish.

Salt and pepper, to taste

400 grams eggplant, sliced lengthwise

Olive oil, for frying the eggplant

150 grams ricotta cheese

Red chili flakes, to taste

50 grams Grana Padano cheese, grated

1 egg

4 servings (approx. 250 grams) Marinara Sauce (see page 29)

50 grams mozzarella, grated

Fresh basil, chopped, for garnish

Fresh parsley, chopped, for garnish

1   Preheat the oven to 390°F. Salt the eggplant and leave for 30 minutes in a colander to draw out the moisture and bitterness.

2   Pat dry the eggplant slices. Pan fry or roast the slices in the oven until cooked and softened, but firm enough to roll.

3   In a bowl, mix the ricotta cheese, salt, pepper, red chili flakes, Grana Padano, and the egg. Place the filling on one end of an eggplant slice and roll the eggplant up lengthwise, forming a roll.

4   Layer a casserole dish with the sauce, then the stuffed eggplant. Top with more sauce and then the mozzarella.

5   Bake for 15 minutes or until the cheese melts. Garnish with the basil and parsley and serve immediately.

SERVINGS: 4
PREP TIME: 10 Minutes
COOKING TIME: 30 Minutes

NUTRITION INFO:
(per serving)

CALORIES: 241
NET CARBS: 5 g
CARBS: 9 g

FAT: 18 g
PROTEIN: 14 g
FIBER: 4 g

EGGPLANT PARMESAN

Once I included my Chicken Parmesan, I knew I had to do the eggplant version as well. I love how meaty eggplant is and, honestly, when you eat this you really don't miss the meat at all. If you're vegetarian, you'll definitely be adding this to your weekly meal plan.

Salt, to taste

300 grams eggplant, sliced

Olive oil, for frying the eggplant

200 grams Marinara Sauce
(see page 29)

50 grams Parmesan cheese, grated

150 grams mozzarella cheese, grated

Fresh basil, for garnish

1 Preheat the oven to 390°F. Salt the eggplant and leave for 30 minutes in a colander to draw out the moisture and bitterness. Pat dry and pan fry (about 4 minutes on each side) until tender.

2 In an ovenproof dish, layer the sauce, Parmesan, eggplant, mozzarella, more eggplant, more sauce, and more Parmesan cheese, much like a lasagna.

3 Bake for 15 to 20 minutes until golden brown, garnish with fresh basil, and serve.

SERVINGS: 1
PREP TIME: 5 Minutes
COOKING TIME: 10 Minutes

NUTRITION INFO:
(per serving)

CALORIES: 426
NET CARBS: 7 g
CARBS: 8 g

FAT: 38 g
PROTEIN: 15 g
FIBER: 1 g

FETTUCCINI ALFREDO

For the longest time in India, most local cafés and restaurants only served two kinds of pastas: red, and white. The red was marinara or arrabiata sauce with an Indian twist; the white a floury béchamel sauce. This version of fettuccini alfredo is a tribute to the "white pasta" we know and love in India.

2 mushrooms, chopped

5 grams garlic, pressed

1 tablespoon olive oil

100 grams zucchini noodles

30 grams Parmesan cheese, grated

30 ml heavy cream

½ teaspoon salt

½ teaspoon pepper

2 thin strips bacon, cooked and chopped, for garnish

Fresh parsley, chopped, for garnish

1 Fry the mushrooms and garlic in the olive oil. Once the mushrooms have released their liquid and any additional liquid has evaporated, add the zucchini and cook for a minute.

2 Add in the cheese and cream and cook until the mixture becomes sauce-like in texture. Season with salt and pepper.

3 Serve garnished with chopped bacon and parsley.

SERVINGS: 2
PREP TIME: 5 Minutes
COOKING TIME: 10 Minutes

NUTRITION INFO:
(per serving)

CALORIES: 263
NET CARBS: 7 g
CARBS: 11 g

FAT: 20 g
PROTEIN: 13 g
FIBER: 4 g

MUSHROOM
RISOTTO

I created this recipe after discovering riced cauliflower during my initial days on keto. I didn't really like cauliflower, so I wanted to find a way to mask its taste and flavor. This recipe did the trick. The flavors of mushroom, garlic, and parsley are what really stand out, with the cauliflower serving as a milky backdrop to it all, giving it the feel of a true risotto.

1 tablespoon butter

10 grams garlic, minced

Salt and pepper, to taste

100 grams mushrooms, sliced

250 grams cooked cauliflower rice (see page 149)

50 grams Parmesan cheese, grated

50 ml heavy cream

1 teaspoon fresh parsley, chopped, for garnish

1 Melt the butter in a pan, then add the garlic and pepper.

2 Once the garlic starts to brown, add mushrooms and cook until they begin to brown. Add the cauliflower rice and mix well.

3 Add the Parmesan and cream, mix well, and cook for 2 minutes.

4 Sprinkle with the fresh parsley and serve.

SERVINGS: 1

PREP TIME: 5 Minutes

COOKING TIME: 5 Minutes

NUTRITION INFO:

(per serving)

CALORIES: 356

NET CARBS: 2 g

CARBS: 3 g

FAT: 35 g

PROTEIN: 8 g

FIBER: 1 g

PESTO SPAGHETTI

This is the easiest and fastest dish you'll ever make. The best part is there is zero compromise on the flavor thanks to the pesto.

1 tablespoon olive oil

100 grams zucchini noodles

1 tablespoon Basil Pesto (see page 22)

20 grams Parmesan cheese, grated, plus more for garnish

Pine nuts, for serving

1 Heat the olive oil in a pan until hot, then add the zucchini noodles. Cook until tender, then add the pesto.

2 Mix well and add cheese to the pan.

3 Turn off the stove and serve with additional Parmesan and some pine nuts.

SERVINGS: 1	**NUTRITION INFO:**	**CALORIES:** 301	**FAT:** 18 g
PREP TIME: 10 Minutes	(per serving for crust)	**NET CARBS:** 8 g	**PROTEIN:** 22 g
COOKING TIME: 35 Minutes		**CARBS:** 14 g	**FIBER:** 6 g

CAULIFLOWER PIZZA

When I was told I could eat pizza on keto, I didn't believe it. When I was told it would be made of cauliflower, I properly scoffed. Then I tested it myself and couldn't believe how good it was. This was one of the recipes that actually encouraged me to start uploading keto recipe videos on my YouTube channel. After all, how could I not share this magic with the world?

250 grams cauliflower, florets separated from stems

Salt and pepper, to taste

15 grams cream cheese

30 grams Parmesan cheese, grated

1 egg

2 tablespoons Marinara Sauce (see page 29)

50 grams mozzarella cheese, grated

30 grams salami, sliced thin

1 Preheat the oven to 375°F. Blitz the cauliflower florets in the food processor until they are the consistency of fine couscous. Cook the blitzed cauliflower in a dry pan for about 5 to 6 minutes over medium heat until cooked through. Transfer to a dry cloth or tea towel and squeeze out all the excess moisture.

2 In a bowl, mix the cauliflower, salt, pepper, cream cheese, Parmesan, and egg.

3 On a baking sheet lined with parchment paper, place your cauliflower dough and shape it into a circle. Bake in the oven for 20 minutes. Remove from the oven, flip over, and layer with sauce, mozzarella, and salami (or other toppings).

4 Return to the oven, bake until the cheese is fully melted, and serve.

SERVINGS: 1
PREP TIME: 5 Minutes
COOKING TIME: 25 Minutes

NUTRITION INFO:
(per serving for crust)

CALORIES: 705
NET CARBS: 10 g
CARBS: 15 g

FAT: 57 g
PROTEIN: 38 g
FIBER: 5 g

FATHEAD CRUST PIZZA

Cauliflower pizza is great but it can be a bit finicky to make. This crust definitely rivals (and probably beats out) the cauliflower crust thanks to its crispy finish and filling ingredients. It's also much easier to make, but the calorie and carb count may just put the cauliflower crust back in the lead. Try both and see which you like best.

100 grams mozzarella cheese, grated

25 grams cream cheese

1 teaspoon garlic bread seasoning

Salt, to taste

50 grams almond flour

1 egg

Marinara Sauce (see page 29)

Toppings of choice

1 Preheat the oven to 390°F. Add the mozzarella and cream cheese to a bowl and microwave for 1 minute. Mix well, add in the seasonings and almond flour, and mix again.

2 Microwave for another 30 seconds and let cool slightly. Then, add the egg and mix well.

3 Roll out the dough between two sheets of parchment paper, or pat into a circle with wet hands.

4 Place on a baking sheet and bake for 15 minutes. Once baked, remove from the oven and flip the base over.

5 Top with sauce and toppings of choice and return to the oven. Broil until the cheese is melted, slice, and serve.

SERVINGS: 2	NUTRITION INFO:	CALORIES: 417	FAT: 26 g
PREP TIME: 5 Minutes	(per serving)	NET CARBS: 1 g	PROTEIN: 36 g
COOKING TIME: 20 Minutes		CARBS: 2 g	FIBER: 1 g

MEATZZA

I made this for a local band called Undying Inc back in 2012. This was during my pre-keto days when the only way to beat the glory of the Bacon Bomb (see page 133) was to make a pizza entirely out of meat. I decided to bring its meaty glory back into the fold for this book.

250 grams ground chicken, beef, or pork

Salt and pepper, to taste

1 teaspoon garlic bread seasoning

1 teaspoon olive oil

1 tablespoon Basil Pesto (see page 22)

10 grams mushrooms, sliced

75 grams mozzarella cheese, grated

20 grams pepperoni

1. Season the ground meat with salt, pepper, and garlic bread seasoning. Mix well and set aside.

2. Add the olive oil to a cold pan and press the meat into the pan in the shape of a pizza. Press until about ½-inch thick.

3. Fry over high heat until the chicken is almost cooked all the way through. Transfer the crust to a wire rack.

4. Spread the pesto on top. Then, add the mushrooms, cheese, and pepperoni (or toppings of choice).

5. Transfer the rack to the oven and broil on high for 10 minutes, or until the cheese is melted and browned. Remove and serve.

DESSERTS

THESE RECIPES AREN'T MINE ALONE. My wife is an exceptional baker and the mastermind behind the best of these recipes. She's taught me the most important lesson when it comes to desserts: baking is a science. While I might be the kind of chef who likes to wing it in the kitchen, it doesn't quite work with sweet treats. So when you make these recipes, the scale is your friend. Be sure to measure things out as per the recipe, keep tweaks to a minimum, and they will all work out. Since everyone has a preference for the kind of sweetener they use, it's always important to taste your cake batters and desserts as you go, because you might need to adjust sweetness to your liking. Happy baking!

SERVINGS: 1
PREP TIME: 2 Minutes
COOKING TIME: 5 Minutes

NUTRITION INFO:
(per serving for cake)

CALORIES: 395
NET CARBS: 4 g
CARBS: 11 g

FAT: 36 g
PROTEIN: 12 g
FIBER: 7 g

NUTRITION INFO:
(per serving for ganache)

CALORIES: 125
NET CARBS: 2 g
CARBS: 3 g

FAT: 18 g
PROTEIN: 1 g
FIBER: 1 g

ALMOND FLOUR MUG CAKE

Baking can be intimidating—all the exacting measures, recipes that you have to follow to the letter, and the many, many variables that can go wrong. This recipe is for the folks who just want a quick and easy dessert that doesn't require much cooking experience, but still gives you a fantastic result.

For the Almond Flour Mug Cake

1 teaspoon melted butter

1 teaspoon heavy cream

1 egg

¼ teaspoon vanilla extract

25 grams almond flour

2 teaspoons unsweetened cocoa powder

A pinch of salt

Stevia, to taste

Whipped cream, for topping (optional)

Sliced strawberries, for topping (optional)

For the Chocolate Ganache

10 grams 85% or higher dark chocolate

10 grams butter

1 teaspoon heavy cream

Stevia, to taste

FOR THE CAKE

Whisk all the wet ingredients, then add the dry ingredients and whisk until smooth. Microwave for 1 minute for a softer texture or 1 minute and 10 seconds for a cakier texture.

FOR THE GANACHE

Break the chocolate into pieces, mix with butter, and microwave for 20 seconds. Add the cream and stevia, mix well, and serve over the mug cake with whipped cream and strawberries, if desired.

SERVINGS: 1
PREP TIME: 5 Minutes
COOKING TIME: 15 Minutes

NUTRITION INFO:
(per serving, includes toppings)

CALORIES: 627
NET CARBS: 10 g
CARBS: 15 g

FAT: 55 g
PROTEIN: 12 g
FIBER: 5 g

BERRY MUG CAKE

Use this recipe to turn a plain vanilla mug cake into a very berry treat that pairs perfectly with the vanilla mascarpone frosting.

For the Berry Compote

100 grams blackberries, pureed and strained

100 grams raspberries, pureed and strained

2 teaspoons erythritol

For the Vanilla Mascarpone Frosting

25 grams mascarpone cheese, at room temperature

25 ml heavy cream

¼ teaspoon vanilla extract

Stevia, to taste

For the Mug Cake

1 teaspoon coconut flour

½ teaspoon baking powder

2 teaspoons berry compote

1 teaspoon heavy cream

2 teaspoons butter

Stevia, to taste

1 egg

1 To make the berry compote, add the pureed berries and erythritol to a saucepan. Heat on a low flame stirring occasionally until you are left with a sticky, jam-like mixture. Set aside and let cool.

2 To make the frosting, whisk all the ingredients until you get a thick frosting. Pour the mixture a piping bag and chill until ready to use.

3 To make the mug cake, add all ingredients to a mug or ramekin and whisk until combined.

4 Microwave for 2½ to 3 minutes at the highest setting, or bake at 345°F for 10 minutes, or until a toothpick inserted comes out clean.

5 Top with the frosting and serve warm or cooled.

SERVINGS: 2
(1 serving = 1 cake and ½ ganache)
PREP TIME: 5 Minutes
COOKING TIME: 5 Minutes

NUTRITION INFO:
(per serving for cake)

CALORIES: 218
NET CARBS: 3 g
CARBS: 8 g

FAT: 17 g
PROTEIN: 5 g
FIBER: 5 g

NUTRITION INFO:
(per serving for ganache)

CALORIES: 156
NET CARBS: 1 g
CARBS: 3 g

FAT: 21 g
PROTEIN: 3 g
FIBER: 2 g

COCONUT FLOUR MICROWAVE MUG CAKE

There are times when you just want a simple yellow sponge or white cake that you can customize. Coconut flour provides the perfect canvas for a vanilla cake, and you can add whatever toppings or frostings you want.

For the Cake

30 grams coconut flour

30 grams butter

2 teaspoons coconut milk

½ teaspoon vanilla extract

¼ teaspoon baking powder

1 egg

Stevia, to taste

A pinch of salt

For the Ganache

15 grams butter or cocoa butter

15 grams peanut butter
(natural and with no sugar added)

1 teaspoon unsweetened
cocoa powder

Stevia, to taste

1 teaspoon coconut milk

1 To make the mug cake, mix all ingredients in a bowl or in a mug and microwave for 90 seconds.

2 For the ganache, microwave the butter and peanut butter for 1 minute and mix until melted. Then, add in the cocoa powder and stevia and mix well.

3 Add the coconut milk, mix, and pour over the mug cake before serving.

NUTRITION INFO:
(per serving)

CALORIES: 294
NET CARBS: 3 g
CARBS: 5 g

FAT: 28 g
PROTEIN: 7 g
FIBER: 2 g

COFFEE MUG CAKE

My wife gets annoyed with my habit of introducing coffee into everything I make, but I can't help it—I love the stuff. There's something about coffee-flavored desserts that makes them perfectly balanced. It's a flavor for all seasons, and this mug cake captures coffee at its best.

For the Cake:

15 grams butter

30 ml heavy cream

1 teaspoon powdered erythritol

1 teaspoon instant coffee powder

½ teaspoon vanilla extract

A pinch of salt

1 egg

½ teaspoon baking powder

20 grams almond flour

2 teaspoons psyllium husk

1 teaspoon unsweetened cocoa powder

Stevia, to taste

For the Frosting:

25 grams mascarpone cheese

25 ml heavy cream

¼ teaspoon vanilla extract

Stevia, to taste

1   To make the cakes, melt the butter in the microwave. Add in the cream, erythritol, and instant coffee powder and mix well.

2   Microwave another 15 to 20 seconds to dissolve the coffee, if needed.

3   Add the vanilla, a pinch of salt, and egg and mix well. Then, add in the baking powder, almond flour, psyllium husk, cocoa powder, and stevia and mix until you get a smooth batter.

4   Divide the batter between two ramekins or mugs and microwave for a minute each.

5   To make the frosting, whip together all the ingredients.

6   Remove the cakes from the microwave, cool, and top with the frosting.

SERVINGS: 1
PREP TIME: 2 Minutes
COOKING TIME: 2 Minutes

NUTRITION INFO:
(per serving without topping)

CALORIES: 533
NET CARBS: 9 g
CARBS: 16 g

FAT: 47 g
PROTEIN: 21 g
FIBER: 7 g

PEANUT BUTTER MUG CAKE

Let's just come out and say it: all keto breads are cakes, really. I found that a little twist in a peanut butter mug bread would turn it into the most delicious mug cake—think a keto peanut butter cup. This is particularly a hit with kids; top with keto-friendly jam and you have a PB and J cake!

60 grams peanut butter
(natural and with no sugar added)

2 teaspoons unsweetened cocoa powder

1 teaspoon butter, melted

1 egg

1 teaspoon heavy cream

½ teaspoon baking powder

Stevia, to taste

Whipped cream, for garnish

1 Mix together the peanut butter, cocoa powder, melted butter, egg, cream, baking powder, and stevia. Whisk until smooth, then pour into a mug and microwave for 1 minute.

2 Top with whipped cream and serve.

TIP: If the mug cake is too wet when it comes out, give it another 15 seconds in the microwave. Conversely, if it's too dry, cut the cooking time by 15 seconds.

SERVINGS: 8
PREP TIME: 15 Minutes
COOKING TIME: 55 Minutes

NUTRITION INFO:
(per serving)

CALORIES: 301
NET CARBS: 6 g
CARBS: 8 g

FAT: 27 g
PROTEIN: 6 g
FIBER: 2 g

FLOURLESS CHOCOLATE CAKE

My wife used to make the most fantastic triple chocolate mousse cake when we weren't on keto, with a flourless chocolate cake base, and two layers of dark and white chocolate mousse. My favorite part was the flourless bit at the bottom, and being the darling she is, she modified the recipe to turn it into the most decadent, dark, truffle-like keto cake. This one is every choco-holic's dream.

200 grams 85% or higher dark chocolate, broken into even pieces

100 grams butter, cubed, plus more for pan

100 ml heavy cream

4 teaspoons Truvia

4 eggs, yolks and whites separated

A pinch of salt

1   Preheat the oven to 325°F. Butter an 8" cake pan.

2   Mix the chocolate and butter and microwave in short bursts until the chocolate is melted, or melt using a double boiler.

3   Add the cream and Truvia to the chocolate mix and use a handheld electric whisk to mix together.

4   Add the egg yolks, one at a time, whisking until just combined. If the fat separates out, continue whisking until it comes together into a thick, shiny mix.

5   Whisk the egg whites separately with a pinch of salt until stiff peaks form. Fold the egg whites into the chocolate mixture ⅓ at a time until no white streaks remain, then pour the mixture into the cake pan.

6   Bake for about 45 minutes or until the cake is set but the center is still slightly soft.

7   Remove and let cool to room temperature, then chill for at least 4 hours before serving. You can also freeze the cake for a later date.

TIP: Don't worry if the cake sinks as it cools, that is perfectly normal.

SERVINGS: 8 (1 serving = 1 slice of cake)
PREP TIME: 10 Minutes
COOKING TIME: 50 Minutes

NUTRITION INFO:
(per serving)

CALORIES: 194
NET CARBS: 2 g
CARBS: 3 g

FAT: 18 g
PROTEIN: 6 g
FIBER: 1 g

LEMON AND RICOTTA CAKE

Lemons are tough to come by in India, so every time someone travels, we ask them to bring us back lemons, which my father-in-law did after his last work trip. My father-in-law's heart is bigger than his suitcase—he brought back two dozen giant lemons and inspired this rustic but delicate keto tea cake, which brings a slice of Italian summer to your plate.

80 grams butter

100 grams Sukrin Gold or keto-friendly sweetener of choice

1 teaspoon vanilla extract

3 eggs

150 grams ricotta cheese

Zest and juice of 1 lemon

100 grams almond flour

1 teaspoon baking powder

Slivered almonds, for garnish

Lemon slices, for garnish

1   Preheat your oven to 320°F.

2   In a large bowl, cream together the butter, sweetener, and vanilla extract. If using a granulated sweetener, make sure to grind to a fine powder before using.

3   Once mixed, add in the eggs one at a time and beat well until frothy.

4   Add in the ricotta cheese, lemon juice, and zest and continue whisking. Don't be alarmed if the mixture looks curdled or split, this is normal.

5   Sift the almond flour and baking powder together in a bowl, making sure there are no lumps. Add the dry ingredients to the wet in two batches and whisk until incorporated.

6   Grease a 8" cake pan and line with parchment paper. Pour in the cake batter, level the top, and place in the oven.

7   Cook for about 50 minutes or until a toothpick inserted comes up with only a few crumbs.

8   Allow the cake to cool before removing from the cake pan. Garnish with slivered almonds and lemon slices, cut, and serve.

SERVINGS: 8 (1 serving = 1 slice of cake)
PREP TIME: 15 Minutes
COOKING TIME: 60 Minutes

NUTRITION INFO:
(per serving)

CALORIES: 301
NET CARBS: 5 g
CARBS: 8 g

FAT: 28 g
PROTEIN: 7 g
FIBER: 3 g

BERRY SWIRL CHEESECAKE

Cheesecake is one of my wife's favorite things to make. This one combines the freshness of berries and the tang of lemon into a beautiful dessert that won't ruin your macros. If you love New York-style baked cheesecake, you'll definitely be dreaming about this.

1 For the berry puree, put the berries in a saucepan over low heat. Add the sweetener, if using, and salt and allow the mixture to reduce until it reaches a jam-like consistency. Set aside to cool.

2 For the base, preheat the oven to 350°F. In a bowl, add the almond flour, sweetener, and salt and mix. Stir in the butter and mix until it forms a dough. Press the dough into a parchment-lined and greased 8" cake pan, level, bake for 10 minutes, remove from the oven, and let cool.

3 To make the filling, heat the oven to 325°F.

4 In a bowl, whisk the cream cheese, mascarpone, and sweetener together until lump-free. Don't over-whisk or the cheesecake will crack later.

5 Add the citrus juice and whisk until just combined, then add the eggs one at a time and whisk until just incorporated. Add the vanilla, whisk, and adjust the sweetener if needed.

6 Divide the cheesecake filling into two parts. Stir the berry puree into one part, then, alternating mixes, add the filling to the cake tin.

7 Shake very gently to level, then bake for 35 to 40 minutes, or until the sides are set but the center is still slightly soft.

8 Remove from the oven and let cool to room temperature on a wire rack. Garnish with strawberries. Then, place in the refrigerator for at least four hours before serving.

For the Berry Puree

200 grams fresh or thawed frozen berries of choice, pureed and strained

½ teaspoon granulated sweetener (optional)

A pinch of salt

For the Base

96 grams almond flour

½ teaspoon granulated sweetener, or to taste

A pinch of salt

50 grams butter, melted

For the Filling

226 grams cream cheese, at room temperature

200 grams mascarpone cheese, at room temperature

Sweetener of choice, to taste

Juice of 1 lemon or lime

2 eggs, at room temperature

½ teaspoon vanilla extract

Sliced strawberries, for garnish

SERVINGS: 3
PREP TIME: 10 Minutes
COOKING TIME: 25 Minutes

NUTRITION INFO:
(per serving)

CALORIES: 490
NET CARBS: 3 g
CARBS: 7 g

FAT: 49 g
PROTEIN: 8 g
FIBER: 4 g

COFFEE AND CHOCOLATE TART

Coffee, chocolate, and mascarpone is a blessed combo. This tart layers the chocolate ganache and coffee-mascarpone crème on a crisp chocolate-almond flour base for a dessert that will always have you going back for seconds (or thirds).

45 grams almond flour

1 teaspoon unsweetened cocoa powder

Stevia, to taste

1 teaspoon vanilla extract

30 grams salted butter, melted

1 teaspoon instant espresso powder

2 tablespoons hot water

150 grams mascarpone cheese

100 ml heavy cream

30 grams 85% or higher dark chocolate

Sea salt, for topping

1 Mix together the almond flour, cocoa powder, stevia, vanilla, and butter until the mixture has the consistency of wet sand.

2 Divide the mixture between three tart tins (about 4") or ramekins and press into the base. Bake the tart crusts at 350°F for 10 minutes and allow to cool.

3 Dissolve the instant espresso powder in the hot water and let cool.

4 Whisk together the mascarpone cheese, additional stevia, and coffee mixture until nice and fluffy. Pour the mascarpone mixture over the cooled tart bases and chill for 15 minutes.

5 Meanwhile, microwave the heavy cream for 30 seconds. Add the chocolate and more stevia and mix until you have a creamy ganache. Pour the ganache over the coffee-mascarpone crème and chill for an hour.

6 Finish with sea salt on top of each tart and enjoy.

SERVINGS: 4
PREP TIME: 5 Minutes
COOKING TIME: 2 Minutes

NUTRITION INFO:
(per serving)

CALORIES: 239
NET CARBS: 2 g
CARBS: 6 g

FAT: 22 g
PROTEIN: 3 g
FIBER: 4 g

CHOCOLATE MOUSSE

When I was growing up, dessert options in most restaurants were limited to Indian sweets, something called a "sizzling brownie with ice cream," or the standard chocolate mousse. Consequently, my childhood was spent eating an extraordinary number of chocolate mousses, and this recipe came about as a big bite of sweet, creamy nostalgia.

50 grams 85% or higher dark chocolate

15 grams butter

200 ml heavy cream

1 teaspoon cocoa powder

Stevia, to taste

1   Melt the chocolate and butter in the microwave for about 30 seconds and mix. Let cool.

2   Whip together the cream, cocoa powder, and stevia, add in the chocolate-and-butter mixture, and whip until soft peaks form.

3   Divide the mousse into serving bowls, then chill for at least an hour before serving.

SERVINGS: 4	NUTRITION INFO:	CALORIES: 146	FAT: 14 g
PREP TIME: 5 Minutes	(per serving)	NET CARBS: 2 g	PROTEIN: 3 g
COOKING TIME: 35 Minutes		CARBS: 3 g	FIBER: 1 g

ETON MESS

This English tuck shop staple is a delicious way to use up broken or failed meringue. Layers of chewy meringue complement the incredible combination of strawberries and cream—and it looks great, too.

2 egg whites

¼ teaspoon cream of tartar

1 teaspoon vanilla extract

1½ teaspoons powdered erythritol

150 ml heavy cream

Stevia, to taste

100 grams strawberries, diced, plus more for garnish

1 Preheat the oven to 245°F. Whip the egg whites until frothy and add the cream of tartar.

2 Continue to whip until the mixture begins to form soft peaks, then add half the vanilla extract and all the erythritol and whip until soft peaks form.

3 Transfer the mixture to a parchment-lined baking sheet and bake for 30 to 35 minutes until cooked through. Allow to cool for 15 minutes before removing from the parchment paper.

4 In a bowl, add the heavy cream, stevia, and the remaining vanilla and whip until soft peaks form. Let chill in the fridge.

5 Fold the strawberries into the chilled cream, then break the meringue and add it to the mixture. Transfer to individual serving bowls or glasses and garnish with half a strawberry.

SERVINGS: 8
PREP TIME: 10 Minutes
COOKING TIME: 5 Minutes

NUTRITION INFO:
(per serving)

CALORIES: 308
NET CARBS: 5 g
CARBS: 6 g

FAT: 29 g
PROTEIN: 16 g
FIBER: 1 g

KETO TIRAMISU

I love nothing more than a well-made tiramisu. When I first got on Keto, my wife came up with this recipe to help with my cravings. Can you believe you can eat tiramisu and lose weight? I still can't.

60 ml espresso

30 ml whiskey (optional)

30 ml heavy cream

1 egg, yolk and white separated

Stevia or keto-friendly sweetener of choice, to taste

400 grams mascarpone cheese

2 portions 90-Second Mug Bread (see page 35)

2 teaspoons unsweetened cocoa powder

1 Mix the espresso, whiskey, and cream to make the soaking liquid.

2 Whisk the egg white to stiff peaks and set aside. Then, whisk the yolk and sweetener until it turns a pale yellow.

3 Add the mascarpone cheese and 60 ml of the soaking liquid to the beaten yolk and whisk until it forms a smooth, custard-like cream.

4 Fold the beaten egg white into the custard mixture in two batches.

5 Slice the bread into circles or fingers depending on the serving dish size, then dip them in the soaking liquid and layer it on the bottom of your dish.

6 Pour the custard over the bread and chill until set. Dust with cocoa powder before serving.

NUTRITION INFO:
(per serving)

CALORIES: 204
NET CARBS: 3 g
CARBS: 3 g

FAT: 20 g
PROTEIN: 3 g
FIBER: 0 g

PANNA COTTA

A well-made panna cotta has the slightest wobble—it should gently shimmy when you shake it—and a texture that absolutely melts in your mouth. Using real vanilla makes a huge difference; none of the store-bought extracts come close to that sweetness and fragrance of the real thing. This classic Italian favorite is something even the most inexperienced home cook can make, as well as one of my personal favorites.

3 grams gelatin

2 tablespoons water

112 ml light or heavy cream

Stevia or keto-friendly sweetener, to taste

1 whole vanilla bean

Mixed berries, for topping

1   Add the gelatin to the water and allow to sit for 5 minutes.

2   Pour the cream into a small saucepan and set it over low heat. Add in the sweetener and stir until dissolved.

3   Slit the vanilla bean down the center and, using the tip of the knife, scrape the seeds from the vanilla pod and add to the cream, followed by the pod.

4   Once the cream begins to simmer, take it off the heat. Discard the vanilla pod, leaving just the seeds. Add the gelatin mixture to the cream and mix well until completely dissolved.

5   Pour into molds and chill in the refrigerator for at least 4 hours.

6   To unmold the panna cotta after they are set, dip the molds halfway into a bowl of hot water, then upend onto a plate. Serve topped with mixed berries.

TIP: To make coffee panna cotta, add a teaspoon of instant coffee granules to each mold in Step 5 and stir into the hot cream.

NUTRITION INFO:
(per serving without topping)

CALORIES: 345
NET CARBS: 6 g
CARBS: 10 g

FAT: 34 g
PROTEIN: 5 g
FIBER: 4 g

POT DE CRÈME

Every once in a while, I'll get a hankering for an intense chocolate dessert. I'd never heard of this French chocolate pot until my wife whipped it up one day; now it's a staple dessert at our house. You can serve this warm or, if you're more patient than I am, wait for it to set in the refrigerator, where it becomes a chocolate truffle.

60 grams 90% or 100% baking chocolate

1 egg yolk

80 ml heavy cream, plus more as needed

1½ teaspoons powdered erythritol

A few drops of vanilla extract

A pinch of salt

Whipped cream or crème fraîche, for topping (optional)

Berry compote, for topping (optional)

1   Break up chocolate into small pieces and place in a bowl. In a separate bowl, add the egg yolk and give it a quick whisk.

2   In a thick-bottomed saucepan, add the cream, erythritol, and vanilla and heat over a low flame, stirring constantly until it reaches a boil. As soon as bubbles appear in the cream, take it off the heat.

3   Add a spoonful of the hot cream to the egg yolk and whisk to temper the yolk, then add the tempered mixture into the saucepan and put over low heat to form a custard.

4   Stir the custard until it starts to thicken. The custard is done when it just coats the back of a spoon.

5   Remove the custard from heat and pour it over the chocolate pieces with a pinch of salt. Let sit for a minute, then whisk until you get a thick pudding. If the chocolate is too thick, add cream to loosen it up.

6   Divide the pudding into two ramekins or cups and enjoy immediately, or chill in the refrigerator for 30 minutes. If desired, top with whipped cream, crème fraîche, or berry compote before serving.

METRIC CONVERSIONS

U.S. Measurement	Approximate Metric Liquid Measurement	Approximate Metric Dry Measurement
1 teaspoon	5 ml	5 g
1 tablespoon or ½ ounce	15 ml	14 g
1 ounce or ⅛ cup	30 ml	29 g
¼ cup or 2 ounces	60 ml	57 g
⅓ cup	80 ml	76 g
½ cup or 4 ounces	120 ml	113 g
⅔ cup	160 ml	151 g
¾ cup or 6 ounces	180 ml	170 g
1 cup or 8 ounces or ½ pint	240 ml	227 g
1½ cups or 12 ounces	350 ml	340 g
2 cups or 1 pint or 16 ounces	475 ml	454 g
3 cups or 1½ pints	700 ml	680 g
4 cups or 2 pints or 1 quart	950 ml	908 g

INDEX

ACKNOWLEDGMENTS

I've spent most of my life chasing the still elusive dream of being a full-time metal musician. Never in a million years did I imagine I'd be authoring my own cookbook, let alone a keto one. First, I cannot thank my family enough; without them I never would have loved food the way I do. I never would have stepped into a kitchen and never been able to write this book.

I have my mom and dad, Vanita and Micky Makhija, to thank, who always fed me well—perhaps too well—and took me to new places to try new foods, and for their constant encouragement, be it following my aspiration to be a chef when I was 10 years old, or my ambition to be a metal musician. I was given nothing but complete freedom to follow my path and their support on the journey was indefatigable.

My late grandfather Ishoo Advani and my grandmother Janki Makhija were absolute legends in the kitchen and passed on a lot of their wisdom to me. If I am even half the cook they were, I will consider myself truly fortunate.

My brother Shome, who sacrificed his space for my music, without which I wouldn't be here, and who later helped me film my YouTube series Bacon Tadka, from which many great ideas were born.

There is no adequate way to say thank you to my wife, Deepti Unni, because I wouldn't be anything without her. She has been my pillar of support, my teacher, my guide, my critic, and my best friend. From taking me to Italy and France to discover new foods to helping me become a better writer and food photographer, she is as much a part of this book as I am. After all, if it wasn't for her doing keto and then passing on all her wisdom and experience to me, I'd never had started developing recipes.

This book took a lot out of me. All of the cooking for this book was done in six days, and those were the hardest six days of my life. I was able to do it because I could bank on my team. Thanks are due to Sunil Thakkar, my long-time school friend, who took all the photographs for the book. And to Alok Verma, my new friend, who styled all the dishes and made everything look so beautiful.

I'm deeply thankful to everyone at Cider Mill Press—John, Buzz, and the entire team—for bringing this book to life and having faith in what I do.

Finally, thank you to the fans who have pushed me with constant messages asking me for this book. It was the motivation I needed to make it happen. This one is for you!

ABOUT THE AUTHOR

SAHIL MAKHIJA's mission to show people how the keto diet can be easy, tasty, and achievable has earned him over 300,000 YouTube subscribers. Keep up with him at headbangerskitchen.com.

Photographs on pages 20, 23-24, 27-28, 31, 34, 37-38, 41-42, 45-46, 50, 53-54, 57-58, 61-62, 65-66, 69-70, 73, 76, 79-80, 83-84, 87-88, 91-92, 95-96, 99-100, 103-104, 107, 110, 113-114, 117-118, 121-122, 125-126, 129, 132, 135-136, 139-140, 143-144, 147-148, 151-152, 155-156, 159-160, 163-164, 167-168, 171-172, 175-176, 179-180, 183-184, 187-188, 191-192, 195-196, 199-200, 204, 207-208, 211-212, 215-216, 219-220, 223-224, 227-228, and 231 styled by Alok Verma and photographed by Sunil Thakkar.

All other photographs used under official license from Shutterstock.com

ABOUT CIDER MILL PRESS BOOK PUBLISHERS

Good ideas ripen with time. From seed to harvest, Cider Mill Press brings fine reading, information, and entertainment together between the covers of its creatively crafted books. Our Cider Mill bears fruit twice a year, publishing a new crop of titles each spring and fall.

"Where Good Books Are Ready for Press"

VISIT US ON THE WEB AT
www.cidermillpress.com

OR WRITE TO US AT
PO Box 454
12 Spring St.
Kennebunkport, Maine 04046